"How to Hire a Cha[mpion]
thought provoking. It has [...]
reader in multiple positions—that of candidate, hiring
manager, CEO, and coworker—so as to provide 360 degree
insight into the optimal hiring process. Moreover, its emphasis on character, self-competition, and persistence raise it to
another level—one of guidance and inspiration for the same
360 degree set of individuals. It is a book to be read again for
its deeper meanings. I recommend it to all and especially to
my children."

—Peter C. Johnson, MD, President and
CEO, Scintellix, LLC

"David's insight into what it takes to hire a champion
challenges much of the prevailing wisdom. He looks at
character and competency in individuals in novel ways that
provide you a different basis for decision-making. His detailed analysis of what a champion is gives you concrete tools
you can use today to improve your interviewing skills and
your hiring processes."

—Rick Rocchetti, Organization Development
and Training Manager, City of Raleigh,
North Carolina

"David's whole philosophy of 'Picking the Best and
Challenging the Rest' is backed up by real science, powerful
tools, and insightful metrics. He has helped us increase our
energy level, development, and performance—for the
largest fashion industry trade show in the world."

—Chris McCabe, Vice President, MAGIC,
The Business of Fashion, a division of
Advanstar Communications

"Everyone talks about the importance of metrics today in assessing and selecting teams, but very few people see the big picture the way David does. This book takes extremely critical and complex issues in hiring and makes them amazingly simple. It is a gift."

—Sid Reynolds, CEO, The Signature Agency

How to Hire a Champion

Champion

INSIDER SECRETS
to FIND, SELECT, AND KEEP
GREAT EMPLOYEES

DAVID SNYDER

CAREER
PRESS

Franklin Lakes, NJ

Copyright © 2007 by David Snyder

HOW TO HIRE A CHAMPION

EDITED BY KARA REYNOLDS
TYPESET BY EILEEN DOW MUNSON
Cover design by Lucia Rossman/Digi Dog Design NYC
Printed in the U.S.A. by Book-mart Press

Author jacket photo: Patrick Bedout Photography,
Villeneuve sur Yonne, France.

To order this title, please call toll-free 1-800-CAREER-1 (NJ and Canada: 201-848-0310) to order using VISA or MasterCard, or for further information on books from Career Press.

The Career Press, Inc., 3 Tice Road, PO Box 687,
Franklin Lakes, NJ 07417
www.careerpress.com

Library of Congress Cataloging-in-Publication Data
Snyder, David, 1960-
    How to hire a champion : insider secrets to find, select, and keep great
  employees / by David Snyder.
       p. cm.
  Includes bibliographical references and index.
  ISBN-13: 978-1-56414-964-0
  ISBN-10: 1-56414-964-1
    1. Employee selection. 2. Employees—Rating of. 3. Achievement
  motivation. 4. Employee retention. 5. Organizational effectiveness.
  I. Title. II. Title: Insider secrets to find, select and keep great
  employees.
  HF5549.5.S38S65 2007
  658.3'11--dc22

                                      2007038672

For Jean-Pierre Sakey,
Vivian Snyder,
Jeff West,
Jeff Herman,
and Jessica Hall.

♛

For Yolanda
with Best Wishes,

David

Acknowledgments

I would like to thank the following people who have helped me throughout the past few years as I worked on this manuscript, and as I continued to examine the research on job performance that has laid the groundwork for it.

First, Jean-Pierre (J.P.) Sakey, who in 2004 was the relatively new CEO of Headway Corporate Resources, and who, that June, called me from his cell phone at JFK airport, after having just finished reading my first book, *How to Mind-Read Your Customers*, which talks about the psychology of building better relationships in the workplace with colleagues and customers. Sakey asked if I would help assemble and guide a team of the "best and the brightest" to create an in-depth process for selecting and screening people based on their character strengths. Intrigued by the opportunity, I joined Sakey as an independent, outside business counsel to help him and his colleagues build a corporate and recruiting framework based on character. It was, after all, an offer I found hard to turn down, given the chance to work with a person of Sakey's knowledge and experience (before being asked by the board of Headway to overhaul the company from the ground up, Sakey had helped run North America for Monster.com, and is considered by many to be a pioneer in the field of recruiting and staffing process and technology).

I owe particular gratitude to Jeff West, president of VantagePoint, Inc., in Omaha, Nebraska, who is one of the nation's leading assessment and competency-modeling experts, and an associate with ASSESS Systems (one of the nation's leading industrial psychology firms), which has conducted an extensive amount of research on the competencies and profiles of high-performing individuals in diverse professions. Jeff, who is one of my consulting partners and an expert in the use of assessment tools and assessment best practices, has been an invaluable guide in helping me to truly understand the balance that must constantly be achieved between assessment (the homework part of selection) and wisdom—which is the hard part. Keith McCook, PhD, and Hal Whiting, PhD, were also of invaluable help in sharing with me years' worth of data that ASSESS Systems has collected on the competencies that predict successful performance across industries.

At a critical time in which I needed feedback and guidance, my Headway colleague Dr. Peter Johnson, a renowned consultant in the biomedical industry (as well as an inspired coach) offered invaluable insight and support; Harvard psychologist Dr. Myra White, author of *Follow the Yellow Brick Road*, also offered insights that were validating, encouraging, and uplifting. Rick Rocchetti, manager of organizational development and training for the City of Raleigh, North Carolina, served as an educator, guide, and friend. Dave Donaldson and Raymond Sipperly of Headway Corporation provided enormous levels of friendship and business support as I worked on the content of the tools presented here. Tom Livaccari, a member of the training committee at Merrill Lynch, provided his usual outstanding advice and mentorship.

My good friend Rebecca Dnistran was a perpetual sounding board and advisor in the initial stages of this work, as was Emily Shurr, with whom I worked closely at the Duke University certificate program in nonprofit management. Teresa Spangler, founder and CEO of Creative Leadership Adventures, offered tremendous feedback, support, and wisdom, as did my former Headway colleague Jim Haynes. My good friend and former Headway colleague Jeff Anderson also provided valuable insights. Jeff Raxlin, a senior vice president with AXA Financial Advisors, contributed a great deal of useful commentary and advice as well. Richard Boren, founder of the Training Registry deserves special thanks for his profound advice on best practices in training and service excellence.

Doug Lennick, managing partner of Lennick Aberman Group, coauthor of *Moral Intelligence*, and an executive vice president with Ameriprise (formerly American Express Financial Advisors), was extraordinarily generous with this time and advice, and with sharing research and ideas. And, as usual, the whole Snyder family was there to provide constant positive energy.

There are many other people to thank, as well—so many they are hard to count. In addition to the people just mentioned, many other team members at Headway from coast to coast showed enormous support, enthusiasm, and effort, and modeled on a daily basis the fundamental principles of character that we were researching in the employment marketplace. I owe each and every one of them a word of thanks for their inspiration and education on the quiet principles of goodness and diligence that describe the heart of character itself.

Champions, first and foremost, are defined by their character. But because character is defined by what people do—not by how they feel or what they think—character has to be proved to others every day. Thus, character can never be assumed or accepted as a given. In the context of character, high-performing individuals are essentially individuals with certain noble traits, such as integrity, persistence, self-reliance, a positive attitude, and a strong desire to prove their worth. When asked to prove, demonstrate, or document their history of character at work, high-performing individuals will readily supply the evidence of their excellence—in writing, if asked.

Champions are not as hard to find as some people may lead you to believe.

Usually, you can see champions coming from a mile away.

They're the ones who still have something to prove.

—Taken from Chapter 1

Contents

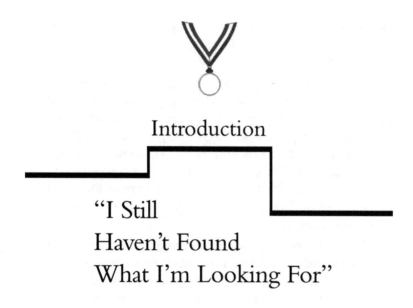

Introduction

"I Still Haven't Found What I'm Looking For"

I have run, I have crawled,
I have scaled these city walls...
But I still haven't found what I'm looking for.

—U2, "I Still Haven't Found
What I'm Looking For"

This book is primarily written for employers—those who are looking for great employees. But it is also useful for job-seekers who want to differentiate themselves from the millions of other people competing for the good jobs out there.

In this book I will attempt to simplify some rather complex issues that affect both successful hiring and successful employment. The nagging question for both employers and job-seekers is the same: "How in the world do I find what I'm looking for?" As we all ponder this question, I often hear the refrain of that great U2 song playing in my head. In my mind's eye, I see a lone Bono, hovering above the world, microphone in hand, belting it out one more time. *I still haven't found what I'm looking for.*

The essential problem for both employers and employees is this: Consumed by overwhelming pressures, and endless demands on our time, we often forget *what* we were looking for in the first place—and that's why we can't find it. This book addresses that problem by sharing tools and processes to help the overworked hiring manager remember the simple goals that matter the most. The primary aim of these tools is to help you find candidates who possess purpose, commitment, and character.

In some ways, the culture of entitlement that is becoming more pervasive every day seems to have created a growing population of people who genuinely think that the world owes them a living, and that they really shouldn't have to work that hard to become super rich and have their every whimsical need satisfied. But somewhere out there is a group of individuals who possess a fierce inner drive to prove themselves, and who would literally bend over backwards to show their employers what they are made of.

People with this coveted mentality—a mentality defined by a passionate inner fire to *prove oneself*—possess a certain noble quality that presents itself at first sight. Because I began this introduction with a reference to Bono and his band, let me continue that thread by sharing a special memory I have of seeing U2 perform live in younger days. Yes, I know it is strange to begin a book about hiring with a rock 'n' roll story, but I think the story might serve as a guiding metaphor of what both employers and stellar candidates are looking for.

Quite a few years ago, I was sitting in the rain with a few thousand other college students on the bleachers of the football stadium at the University of North Carolina at Chapel Hill. Our annual Springfest concert was all washed out. Huddled under umbrellas and plastic sheets, we shivered in the drizzle.

Four or five bands had been on the roster, but most of them had cancelled. Just as everyone else was about to pack up and leave, the announcer came out and said, "The last band on the roster has decided to perform. They will be on in 10 minutes." The band in question had just released their third album, titled *War*, but most people had never heard of the first two albums. Prior to this they had been playing mostly in bars and clubs, and this was to be their first major outdoor concert in America, their first stop on the *War* tour, and a warm-up to the forthcoming US Festival a month later that was to put them on the map forever. By the time they were announced, only a few die-hard students remained. The bleachers looked almost empty. The rain continued to pour. But in 10 minutes exactly, the band took the stage. A very young Bono, cordless microphone in hand, jumped off of the stage onto the rain-soaked football field, and tramped around in the mud, as he launched into an impassioned speech.

"What in the world!" he shouted (or something to that effect), as he worked the crowd like an evangelist. "It's only a little rain. Where we come from, it rains every day! And I want to thank all of you who stayed. Thank you for sitting here in the rain. You're what rock 'n' roll is all about—and we hope we won't disappoint you." After that, he climbed the stage's scaffolding until he was on top of the tarp covering the band and the instruments. From this vantage point, he jumped up and down on the tarp, waving a white flag, while the band launched into a rousing rendition of "New Year's Day." At this point, all the students remaining in the bleachers rose to their feet, and began clapping in the rain, loudly shouting their approval. Although it continued to rain from that point on, no one seemed to notice it anymore. They were transfixed by the spirit of the guy with the flag.

I remember turning to my brother Steve, who had been sitting beside me. "Something tells me these guys are going to be the biggest thing in the business pretty soon," he said.

"I think you're right," I replied.

Through the prism of time, I remember this rain-soaked event as a living metaphor, or parable, of passion—and the kind of exuberance, reliability, resilience, and dedication that define people of purpose who end up leaving a great mark on the world.

There are two key points we can take from this story as we ponder the fact that so many of us—employees and job-seekers alike—still haven't found what we're looking for.

In a very real sense, most employers aren't looking for fancy, slick resumes and job-seekers who come in bringing well-rehearsed speeches and a laundry list of negotiable perks to which they feel they are entitled. What most employers in all professions are looking for is people with professional dedication and *purpose.* In other words, all employers searching for a great employee are in many ways looking for their own professional version of a Bono—someone who doesn't need to be told how high to climb; someone who just instinctively grabs hold of the scaffolding and climbs, inspiring everyone else in the process.

But great employees—the people everyone wants—have their standards too. They want to work for great employers, doing work that brings meaning to their lives. In other words, they want to know that you have a flag to wave. A flag they would be proud to follow.

This principle of duality in the world of successful hiring and successful retention is the glue that will hold the framework of this book together—it is a principle that speaks to the desire of employers to find great employees (to hire champions), and the desire of great candidates to find great employers. You can't have one without the other.

Our discussion in this book will show that there are relatively simple questions you can ask, and relatively simple measures that you can put into place to investigate a person's documented history of displaying **success-oriented** character in the workplace. In order to uncover success-oriented behavior, you can't ask your candidates just any questions about their character. You have to ask them the *right* questions. And it is also not very useful to focus on just any human attributes, or attributes that you *believe* may be related to strong character and success—you must look for traits that we *know* are related to both strong character and success. That, in essence, is the main purpose of this book: to detail the character traits that are important to investigate from a job performance point of view, and to show you the kinds of questions you can ask of your organization, yourself, and your candidates, to better select people who have those traits of success and high performance that you and your organization are looking for, while also making sure that these people provide a proper fit with your own culture.

A few basic tools that are helpful for finding, screening, and selecting employees with outstanding character are:

1. A job description that includes not only the skills that you are looking for, but also an analysis of the kind of *character* you are looking for in the employee—what is it that you are looking for the person to prove to *you*.

2. A precisely worded description of your culture that you can share with candidates.

3. Exercises that require the candidates to share their problem-solving process, track record of accomplishments, and areas of greatest potential contribution.

4. The use of validated, competency-based assessment tools whenever possible. There are online assessment tools that are industry-specific that can help you to benchmark the candidate against other candidates applying for the same position. We will

discuss the usefulness of these tools in subsequent chapters. However, these tools should only be used as a supplement to the screening process, not as final decision-making instruments (we will discuss more of that later).

5.   The assignment of writing tasks or essays wherever possible to get an advance read on the following attributes: the candidate's seriousness and initiative (manifested by doing the assignment in the first place); ability to summarize values and character traits to you ahead of time; ability to articulate values or what lies at the core; critical thinking and analysis skills.

6.   Reference checks that ask questions about workplace competencies or actions related to character.

With this simple template in mind, let's proceed to the first chapter, where we will discuss the foundation of a success-driven mentality, and also cover the process for writing a job description and advertisement that will be more likely to attract candidates with the kind of character you are looking for.

PART I

Understanding, Appreciating, and Evaluating the Character of Top Performers

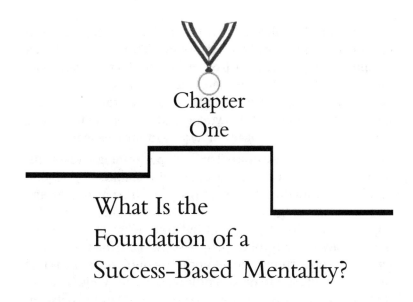

Chapter One

What Is the Foundation of a Success-Based Mentality?

In my experience, successful people—including successful employees and successful managers—are those people who have identified their purpose in life, and who have followed their hearts into careers that capitalize on their strengths. High-performing individuals in any profession, from entry-level to CEO positions, don't really think of their occupations as "jobs"—they see their occupations as an opportunity to make a difference in the world, to help others, and to prove themselves to someone.

Before anyone begins to protest that such a statement is a little too lofty for anything but high-profile or glamorous occupations, let me provide a simple example that may serve to make my point.

My colleagues and I were once working with a call center that wanted to improve hiring and retention for an entry-level position in the mortgage industry. The job paid little more than

$12 an hour. We collected performance data on top performers versus average and low performers. Then we interviewed a sample of employees in each category to see how they felt about their $12-an-hour jobs. The employees who ranked low or average for performance showed little enthusiasm for the job, had nothing much to say about anything, and did not feel they had a close relationship with or much respect for management.

What was odd was this: The high-performing individuals, who worked for the same managers, did feel they had a good relationship with their managers, respected their managers, and viewed their managers as mentors. Moreover, they were highly appreciative of their jobs, and felt their jobs gave them the opportunity to help other people solve their financial problems. This opportunity to help other people made them feel they had the chance to make a difference in the world. In addition to this, we discovered an interesting relationship between the self-reported job satisfaction of these high-performing individuals and the high-performing lending officers who had once been their predecessors. The high-performing lending officers, when asked what they liked about their jobs, said they were close to their managers, felt they were being mentored, and liked having the opportunity to help people and make a difference in the world. They saw their jobs as giving them the chance to do that. And the lower-performing lending officers, who worked for the same managers, didn't have much good to say about them, and also didn't have much enthusiasm for their jobs. They certainly didn't perceive that their jobs gave them the chance to make a difference in the world.

The findings we unearthed in this call-center discovery session reminded me of the results of a study I coauthored with Dr. Scott Dellana of East Carolina University on the relationship between student outlook, grades, and perception of counseling quality in a rural high school (Scott Dellana and David P. Snyder, "Student Future Outlook and Counseling Quality in a Rural Minority High School," *High School Journal*

88(1):27–41, 2004). In that study, we found that students with self-reported higher grades also felt better and more optimistic about the future, and perceived that they were receiving a higher quality of counseling. Students who perceived a lower quality of counseling, and who were making lower grades, were being counseled by the same counselors. This is a highly simplified description of an otherwise complicated study that raised many "chicken and egg" questions regarding optimism and performance, but we can offer a simple observation: People who are optimistic about life (even in a poor, rural area) probably do better in school than people who are not optimistic. And workers who seem to appreciate their jobs and their managers probably perform a lot better on all occasions than people who do not appreciate their jobs or their managers. These principles of optimism and appreciation seem to factor in robustly to what we might call the *character traits* of high-performing individuals—a subject we will be exploring from many different angles during the course of this book.

Following the Yellow Brick Road

Harvard psychologist Dr. Myra S. White, in her book *Follow the Yellow Brick Road: A Harvard Psychologist's Guide to Becoming a Superstar*, examines the factors that make people successful in the workplace. Based on her research on the careers of more than 60 highly successful people—including Jack Welch, former CEO of General Electric; Oprah Winfrey; Warren Buffett; and Lance Armstrong—she states that high achievers have at least four qualities in common: They know their strengths and weaknesses (and pick careers that exploit their strengths), they have clear plans on where they are going, they have a strategy for getting there, and they never forget to have fun, keeping a sense of enthusiasm and joy for the job. Dr. White is a high achiever herself, holding both a Harvard PhD in psychology, and a Harvard Law School degree.

Besides serving as a clinical instructor in the Department of Psychiatry at Harvard Medical School, her company, Behavior Scientific, helps companies identify and develop superstars.

"For successful people," Dr. White has said, "it is not about money or fame. They know that success is really about expressing what is best in each of us in a way that we enjoy, and accomplishing things that add value to the lives of others."

This seems to apply to the business superstars just mentioned, and to other superstars such as Richard Branson of the Virgin Group, Jeff Bezos of Amazon.com, Fred Smith of FedEx, Sam Walton of Wal-Mart, Bill Clinton, Bill Gates, and a host of others whom Dr. White has studied.

The secret of inner outlook also seems to apply to $12-an-hour call-center employees and high-performing students in one of the poorest counties in North Carolina, where there are few jobs. The traits of expressiveness—expressing what we enjoy—and the desire to help others also seem to lie at the core of the character of high-performing individuals.

Thus, basic questions one would ask of potential high-performers could be fairly simple: How did you feel about your last job? How do you feel about the future? How would you like to make a difference in the world? Do you feel that you could do that here? How did you get along with your last managers? Did you feel that they were mentors? What strengths do you bring to the job? Where are you going in your career? How do you plan to get there? How will this help you get there? What will make this opportunity exciting for you? We will examine the simplicity and importance of these types of "character-based" questions in the course of this book.

People Skills, Character, and Science

As we will also demonstrate in portions of this book, validated selection tools demonstrate that such character traits are predictive of high performers in many industries. For example, the industrial psychologists my partners and I work with have found that top performers among banking sales associates possess, among other traits, dependability, self-reliance, resilience, a strong work ethic, and desire to accommodate others. Using screening mechanisms can be powerful. In fact, one validation study demonstrated that when such traits are used as screening mechanisms in the selection process, the percentage of top performers hired was increased by more than 50 percent.

Adding to the list of character traits that predict success, Doug Lennick, an executive vice president of Ameriprise, and his colleagues at Lennick Aberman Group, researched high-performing financial advisors. Results showed that integrity was the key behavioral competency that predicted the most positive returns for clients. This was followed by client service orientation, concern for order/quality, teamwork, self-confidence, achievement orientation, and conceptual (strategic) thinking.

Validated tests can help us get at such traits. But, as we stated, so can the simple type of questions we posed arlier. In the best of all possible worlds, employers will use validated assessments in addition to character-based interviews to help both themselves and their candidates get a better handle on the jobs and situations that are best for the candidate and the employer alike. But we cannot assume that everyone who reads this book will want to invest in the implementation of validated assessment tools and processes for every job, so we will have to proceed as if you were doing all of this on your own, and had to hire champions based on nothing but the simple tools, processes, and questions described on these pages.

All of these processes get at one thing: character.

Why Character Analysis Makes Hiring Easier

Few people would challenge the notion that character is one of the most important components of long-term success in one's career. Other factors may contribute to success—

such as skill, knowledge, talent, and education—but character is what *sustains* success. Character, in essence, is reflected in those personal traits and patterns of behavior that form a lifelong pattern of goal-oriented action. In other words, character is not how we *feel* about things. Character is what we *do* about things. Therefore, character, as reflected in *action*, is often the ultimate predictor of long-term success—much more so than intelligence, experience, or skill.

In this book, I will address and assess current best practices in screening, hiring, and retention. I will also provide pure philosophical insights on the importance of certain character traits that seem to lie at the core of many high-performing individuals. However, I want to make it clear that I do not believe there exists or ever will exist one perfect recipe for successful hiring. That is because human beings are unique and complex. Those individuals with especially strong talents and gifts are not so easily categorized. For example, I have seen individuals who were top performers in their profession score in the average range on professional assessment tests, and I have seen average performers score high. I have seen some companies create elaborate processes for recruiting and selection only to walk away still scratching their heads and asking, *why is it so hard to pinpoint those individuals who will succeed in any given occupation?* Could it be that in some cases we have made the hiring process so complex that we sometimes have a hard time seeing the forest for the trees?

One thing I have noticed in discussing current hiring processes with various companies is this: In many cases, companies continue to add to the complexity of the hiring processes, but often do not give much thought to the factors of their hiring criteria that may be getting in the way. As far as I can tell, the best way to go about constructing a more powerful screening and selection process for top performers is to temporarily lay all thought of existing processes aside and pretend for a moment that you were building your hiring process all over again, from scratch, brick by brick. As part of this thought experiment, you will lay down the most important brick first, and only add to the process when you are convinced that the additional selection tool or assessment strategy will significantly help you to find exactly what you are looking for.

In using a methodical approach to analyzing the strengths and weaknesses of current hiring processes, all roads lead to the person who will be responsible for managing the person who will be hired, and who will ultimately be held accountable for that person's performance.

Managers, Trust Your Knowledge!

No one should understand the job better than the manager whose own job is on the line if the right candidates are not hired, trained, and developed, and if goals are not met. Great managers are able to quickly articulate what the strengths and qualities of their high performers are, because they have taken the time to meticulously study these traits. Also, great managers understand the strengths and weaknesses of the team, and realize that no one individual can possibly succeed without the contributions and support of his or her team members. Therefore, the suggested "success profile" of any individual on the team or any prospective candidate only makes sense if it complements the success profile of the team as a whole. Sales teams provide a great example of this truth. On high-functioning sales teams, different types of salespeople play different roles. Some may be great at going for the highest-hanging fruit and bringing in one or two sales a year—but those sales are worth millions each. Others may lack the skill to go after big-ticket sales, but may be great at pounding the database all day long and bringing in hundreds of smaller sales. This does not mean that one is a better salesperson than another—they are different *types* of salespeople, and the big-ticket salesperson might be indebted to the small-ticket champion for keeping the pipeline alive. That is why all great managers realize the enormous weight of the responsibility that lies on their shoulders where hiring is concerned—they are the ones who understand the chemistry of the team. After all the assessments have been given, and all the skills tests completed, and all of the references checked, and all of the interview questions asked, it is the manager and the manager alone who must answer these questions: Is this person bringing the missing quality or qualities that my *team* needs? Is this person going to make my team more successful? Is this person going to feel successful in the job? Is this really what he or she wants to do?

The most powerful conversations I have had with peers— whether I was on the giving or receiving end of the educational process—always boiled down to this: Remember what you know, and have always known, and keep the basics top of mind. This especially applies to the subject of character. What are the things you have always known to be true about success, character, honor, and courage? What are the things that your candidate has always known to be true about success, character, honor, and courage? Have your candidates been sticking by these principles for most of their lives? Have they demonstrated these principles on the job? And have they used their character-driven principles to inspire and motivate others on the teams they have worked with? If so, how?

Success Is a Team Activity

Success means different things to different people. Here are but a few examples from the behavioral view: Some highly driven people feel most successful if they perceive that they are winning in terms of money—triumphant in an economically competitive sense. Others might feel they are successful if everyone seems to like them. Yet others might feel most successful if they know they are making safe decisions for their company and their clients. Still others might feel that they are most successful as long as they maintain high standards of accuracy. In many cases and many jobs, the ideal individual would be motivated by all of these factors at once. In the sphere of values, some are passionate about research and theory, some are most concerned with improving society, others are passionate about aesthetics and form, and still others are most proud when they have mastered a technical skill. Great managers know that teams most often function best when skill sets and personal qualities are diverse, and when individuals hired feel that they have been carefully chosen for their uniqueness—eccentricities and all.

Great managers also work backward from the standpoint of the customer's view. If your best customer were to analyze your entire company, how would he or she rank you in terms of your reliability, your efficiency, or any other factors that mattered most? Are there any people on the team who seem to personify the behavioral qualities that make you most attractive to the customer? Are there any behavioral qualities that are important to the customer that are *not* personified by at least one person on your team? If so, what? If there were one quality that you could improve at your company in order to strengthen its overall relationship with its customers, what would that be? Is it possible to find that quality in a human being? Are you testing and screening for it now? What would be the first and most important brick to lay down if you were rebuilding your selection process from scratch today?

Laying the First Stones of a Successful Hiring Process

Most managers admit that hiring mistakes are made when they hire too fast. So one of the clues to successful hiring is to *slow down*—and think carefully what may be motivating you or anyone else involved in the hiring process to want to move too quickly.

+ Has the candidate's charm created too much enthusiasm on the part of the hiring team?

+ Has the job been put under a microscope? When was the last time the job description had a check-up? If you have high performers in the same role, do they agree that the job description is as accurate as it can be, and truly reflects the difficulties of the job?

+ Has anyone tried to sell the candidate on the job too fast? In other words, has someone involved in the hiring process made the candidate unrealistically enthusiastic? Has anyone tried to talk the candidate *out of the job* by describing how demanding it is? How did the candidate respond to that? Was the candidate given a fair chance to de-select himself or herself?

+ Have those involved in the hiring process taken the time to thoroughly consider and investigate the character traits that will be needed in the ideal candidate, in addition to the skills?

In examining these issues, there are a few basic elements of process and procedure that can help us to make more enlightened hiring decisions, I believe—decisions that are in the best interest of the employer and the candidate as well.

How Much Process Do You Need to Find the Perfect Fit?

There is much discussion and debate in the human capital industry today about how much process is needed in the hiring of candidates who will ultimately provide the best fit for organizations. Based on my experience, the process for hiring top performers should at least include the following basic steps:

1. Create a respectful hiring environment in which the hiring manager approaches the candidate more as a career counselor than an interrogator. Help the candidate to make the decision about whether the job is right for him or her.

2. Allow candidates to help you with the assessment process. Give them ample opportunity to assess themselves and to help create the conversation that will guide the interview.

3. Use an analysis of character as the blueprint for every stage of the hiring process. Create a process that will enable candidates to show you their character. Give them the chance to talk and write about their character—and to document the parts of their life and career that show evidence of important traits such as persistence, optimism, and resilience. By listening carefully to your candidates' life stories of character, you may discover critical clues about their potential that every skills test and assessment test in the world may have overlooked.

4. If personality or behavioral assessments are used in addition to skills tests, use validated, competency-based assessments that draw from industry-specific data on the predictable benchmarks of top performers in those specific jobs. Use these assessments as a conversation tool to help candidates better understand and talk about their potential strengths and weaknesses in light of the job.

Insider Secret: Character Comes First

In the following I will give "insider secrets" from two professionals who have long put character first in their own hiring and screening practices. The first contribution comes from

Robert Graham, president and CEO of RG Capital of Scottsdale, Arizona, a thriving and rapidly expanding wealth management firm. Robert was honored nationally by being named the Advisor of the Year for 2007 by *Boomer Market Advisor Magazine*. In the proceding section, Graham describes how character has been not only the secret of his own success, but has also been the cornerstone of his hiring practices. He is also executive chairman of iNation, which has created a cutting-edge, Web-based customer relationship management tool for the financial services industry.

♛ ♛ ♛

Pedigree vs. Potential in Hiring Champions
by Robert Graham, CEO, RG Capital;
executive chairman, iNation

RG Capital and iNation, collectively, move at an extremely fast pace. The pace and the performance expectations go way beyond a person's raw and educated talents. Building an "A" team for management and for rank and file employees has proven to be our greatest organizational challenge. In an effort to identify and build a team that would help meet and/or exceed each of our corporate initiatives while staying true to our mission, we have identified the most efficient screening criteria. Our process works to identify traits and/or characteristics that go beyond impressive educational pedigrees. Scott Alexander, the author of *Rhinoceros Success*, defines a hard-charging and success-oriented person as a "Rhino." He further defines the Rhino as someone who has 2-inch-thick skin and is a person who charges through the jungle with a "Damn the torpedoes" mentality. A mentality that means if you get knocked down by some unforeseen challenge, you will get back on your feet and continue charging forward to accomplish your goals.

The hunt for the right employees is long, hard, and risky. Organizationally there are many hardships, challenges, and impenetrable barriers encountered along the way. Corporate-induced turnover, or turnover due to changing market dynamics are painful, time consuming, and costly. The goal for me is to continue building "A" level teams of Rhinos. The traits and characteristics of Rhinos, as defined by Scott Alexander, are synonymous with warriors, leaders, team players, and proclaimed successful individuals. I want people on my team that are not afraid to think for themselves. I search for individuals who are athletic and have the ability to change and adapt to given market dynamics. I look for people who will take calculated risks, apply their thoughts, and face the consequences (good or bad). For an employer, each new hire is a risk. The risk includes financial risk, consumer risk, and interoffice/interpersonal team risk. Finding the right person and/or people has been critical for our success.

When considering a new hire, our formula is simple "P vs. P." Pedigree vs. potential. In our formula, pedigree equals educational pedigree. The second "P" is potential. Potential equals, what is possible with this individual? In some cases we find candidates who are well educated and have an undying motivation to press on and "make things happen." Unfortunately, these type of candidates are rare, and we find our way back to P vs. P. All candidates have to prove their value. Each candidate has to demonstrate through individual and team interviews a history of innovation, ability to overcome adversity, success, and the capacity to maintain excellence.

My team and I test all candidates against the following characteristics and/or traits:

Desire: The candidate must express a sincere interest in our organization, the mission, and the vision. To weed out candidates and to identify candidates to move to the next round of interviews, we assign them a task to read a recommended book, and then we require the candidate to report the top five points of value. There are multiple behavioral traits we are testing: (1) Will they accept work? (2) Do they follow directions? (3) Accountability for the report. (4) How well they communicate the five points. And (5) value alignment. Our current superstars achieve high marks in the aforementioned points.

Courage: The candidate must demonstrate the quality of mind that enables a person to face difficulty, pain, and obstacles, and maintains his or her principles in spite of criticism and/or opposition. We ask, and ask again, for the candidate to articulate well-defined previous experiences that may support these questions.

Process Driven: With an end in mind it is essential for our organizations to systematically accomplish a task or tasks at hand. I have found that true "best practices" are generally a series of actions directed to some end. When a candidate can clearly outline a process or series of actions he or she has performed in order to accomplish a specified objective, we ask him or her to repeat the process in writing. If he or she is able to demonstrate consistency and clear communication, we are off to the next trait.

Endurance: Candidates must carry the capacity to endure. By way of experience and/or recognition, the candidates must be able show a track record that exemplifies "Endurance of Excellence." For example, a sales candidate who is number one for five years running has demonstrated a history of excellence. Candidates who are able to quantify their successes and their continued successes have a lasting quality and an enduring value as it relates to their consideration.

In summary, I have found there is no "perfect" approach. The job market is easily influenced, and trends with many of the geo-economical issues we face as a nation and a shrinking globe. Early on I recognized we have to carry similar traits and qualities as employers. We must have the desire to build, the courage to lead, the processes to achieve, and the endurance to be excellent always. Organizationally we aim for more successes then failures. We accomplish our goal!

The next "insider secret" comes from Paulette Bennett, manager of the Headway Recruiting Center, a high-technology sourcing and recruiting hub that uses state-of-the art tools to locate and screen candidates for both large and small recruiting projects. Looking back at the span of her career, Paulette says that a few basic elements of best practices are key to building a successful process.

❦❦❦

Putting Character First in the Hiring Process
by Paulette Bennett, CTS,
manager, Headway Recruiting Center

I have interviewed thousands of candidates during my career as a recruiter. From this experience, I have learned something salient.

Screening matrices, skills assessments, verification of a candidate's education and employment history, and core competencies are all very important. However, where I have seen the most successful placements is when there is a match between a candidate's values and those of the employer.

Most specific job skills can be learned. On the contrary, basic character, resilience, loyalty, and dedication are difficult to manifest if they have not been learned by the time a person has reached working years. While these attributes can be refined, for the most part they are inherent traits instilled in us as young people. Once we determine if a person can do a particular job, the question then becomes, will he or she be happy and productive, and mesh with the client's corporate culture? Does the candidate possess the core values that match those of the employer? If the candidate does not pass this test, then real concern is raised about the person's appropriateness for the job.

Here are the best techniques I have discovered for assessing character and cultural fit:

- The Magic Question—"Tell me about yourself." I don't ask this question to evoke a response about what position the job-seeker is interested in or what salary he or she is seeking, but I use it to get a feel for the candidate's personality. Is he or she positive, confident, enthusiastic, and outgoing? Does he or she possess less desirable traits, such as critical, negative, and judgmental thought processes?

- Sixth sense—Don't ignore your intuition that tells you something is wrong. Ask probing questions and check references very thoroughly. Dig deep and don't be afraid to challenge the candidate's answers.

- Work history—I ask the candidate why he or she has left each job he or she has held. It is an immediate red flag regarding the candidate's character when he or she begins to talk negatively about former employers.

- Culture—You don't know if you don't ask. Ask the question, "What are you looking for in your ideal employer?"

It has been said that "Character is Destiny." In addition to skills assessment, having the capacity to plumb the character of a candidate may do more for your client than any other recruiter function you provide.

Note that you are making the assumption that the corporate culture is one that values high character. If what you are after is only a match between candidate character and employer culture, this can cover the range from the Mafia to Mother Theresa. You may want to make a statement early on that you work with clients who demand high character of their employees as part of their corporate culture. Then, all of the logic is in sync.

═══════

What Are Your Thoughts on the Character Connection?

Throughout this book, we will continue to discuss the nature of high-performing individuals, and the way their character traits continue to influence their performance and their destiny. There is no formulaic approach here—I will be presenting character and performance from many different angles. Your own thoughts on the character traits that matter most in job performance will be just as important.

An old adage states that the mentality of success is described by the three Ps: perseverance, persistence, and positive attitude. Many high-performing individuals I have met and studied throughout the years indicate that they remember possessing those types of qualities from early childhood.

I know one high-performing individual, for example, who set national records in swimming long before becoming a top-ranked consultant. She vividly remembers waking up at 4:30 a.m. every day when she was 8 years old in preparation for three hours of lap swimming before school. What were the motivations that drove this 8-year-old to push herself so hard? She said that it was because she had to make herself "atypical." She had to "differentiate herself."

But was this inner drive to differentiate herself innate or learned? It was probably a little bit of both, she said. Her personality made her competitive from day one. However, she believes that the character traits of perseverance and persistence were largely shaped and molded by her parents. Although she was born with a desire to be different, it was her parents who continued to reinforce the fact that being successful only happens as the result of continuous hard work.

So throughout the course of her youth, she continued to work relentlessly—setting higher and higher goals, and having those goals encouraged and reinforced by her mentoring parents, who set an example, encouraged her daily, and held her accountable. Although the family was upper middle class, she was never allowed to get by easy, because her parents did not want her to develop a sense of entitlement. She was constantly reminded that the only way to become successful and happy in the world is to find something you love to do, and then prove yourself to be the best at it. The work paid off. She was eventually admitted to virtually every Ivy League school in the country, accepted an offer from Harvard, and became captain of the women's swimming team.

Although many high-performing individuals would describe themselves as being intelligent, few of them would say that their intelligence was the ultimate key to their success. Rather, they would say that their success was mostly a result of their uninterrupted determination to raise the bar and their relentless goal-oriented behavior.

If the process of identifying top performers lies in assessing their perseverance, persistence, and positive attitude, along with any number of skills, competencies, and experiences we require, then we must examine numerous factors that support these traits, competencies, and skills. But of all of the factors we can examine, many of which will be covered in this book, are there any factors that may be more important than the rest?

I have put this question to many leaders in the recruiting profession whom I admire, and most of the time they same the same thing: In the final analysis, what they are looking for is professional fire—or dedication. Sometimes dedication can present itself without emotionalism, but it is always connected with a desire to be professionally better today and tomorrow than one was yesterday.

What Character Traits Matter Most to You?

America was built on character—traits such as determination, optimism, and resilience defined the people who settled this nation. Viewed in this light, the founding fathers and settlers of America, and those who built its great cities and industries, were all high-performing individuals.

One of the main themes of this book is showing how employers can learn to be more discerning in their review of high-potential candidates by critically analyzing the track record of *character* in the people they are about to hire. Unfortunately, not all candidates have the kind of character that America was originally built on, so if high performance is your goal, it is important to put character first when judging the kind of people you want to hire.

But what, exactly, are the building blocks of character? What are the traits that are most important to look for? There may not be a precise answer to this question, but at least some authors and experts have taken a stab at it. For example, consider Senator John McCain and Mark Salter's rich and captivating book *Character is Destiny* (Random House, 2005), in which we are presented with seven essential components of character that are broken down into subcomponents. The seven building blocks of character in McCain and Salter's book are honor, purpose, strength, understanding, judgment, creativity, and love. Under the factor of strength (as just one example), McCain suggests six sub-traits: courage, personified by Edith Cavell (a nurse who lost her own life to a firing squad after helping to save the life of British soldiers in World War I); self-control, personified by George Washington; confidence, personified by Queen Elizabeth I; resilience, personified by Abraham Lincoln; industry, personified by Eric Hoffer (a San Franciscan longshoreman who became a popular writer on social issues); and hopefulness, personified by John Winthrop (a pilgrim settler).

The Josephson Institute of Ethics, a Los Angeles–based nonprofit organization that created the *CharacterCounts!* education initiative, extols trustworthiness, respect, responsibility, fairness, caring, and citizenship as pillars of character and pillars of success in life and business as well.

Such traits and virtues are similar to the character traits of high performers we will be discussing in this book—bedrock character traits that can be observed with the human eye in the form of repeated patterns of diligent behavior, and which seem to be connected with success in one's career. In other words, we will be looking at those factors that seem to make a person more productive, more appealing to one's employers and fellow workers, and more successful in one's chosen vocation.

In laying down a process for hiring that includes an emphasis on character, you may want to consider the following questions, realizing that your own intuitive knowledge and understanding of character is the wellspring of wisdom that will help you make the most of all the data you will collect in the hiring process.

Here are the questions:

—————

- When you think of the employee you had the best experience working with in your career, what was the one character trait that defined this person's attitude?

  _____

- What was the one character trait that defined this person's behavior?

  _____

- What was the one character trait that defined this person's dedication to his or her primary skill set or talent?

  _____

- What was the one character trait that defined this person's relationship to others?

  _____

- What was the one character trait that helped you understand this person's most important motivation in life?

  _____

- What was the one character trait that helped you to understand this person's integrity?

In answering these questions, you have helped to identify what the definition of a "success mentality" is, from your point of view. As we embark on the next chapter, we will continue to explain why your own analysis of character and competency in the context of the jobs you are trying to fill is so important.

Our main theme is this: Champions, first and foremost, are defined by their character. But because character is defined by what people *do*—not by how they feel or what they think—character has to be proved to others every day. Thus, character can never be assumed or accepted as a given. In the context of character, high-performing individuals are essentially individuals with certain noble traits, such as integrity, persistence, self-reliance, a positive attitude, and a strong desire to prove one's worth. When asked to prove, demonstrate, or document their history of character at work, high-performing individuals will readily supply the evidence of their excellence—in writing, if asked.

Champions are not as hard to find as some people may lead you to believe.

Usually, you can see champions coming from a mile away.

They're the ones who still have something to prove.

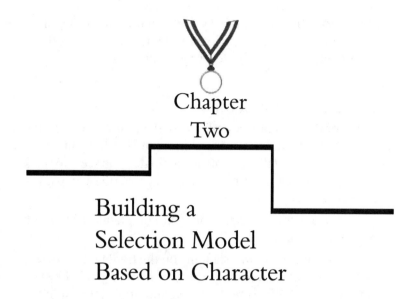

Chapter
Two

Building a
Selection Model
Based on Character

Moral Intelligence: Enhancing Business Performance and Leadership Success by Doug Lennick and Fred Kiel (Wharton School Publishing, 2005), explains how leading companies such as American Express have put a lot of emphasis on screening for character, and then coaching and developing character by focusing on certain traits and aptitudes Lennick and Kiel have defined as "moral intelligence." These traits are: integrity, responsibility, compassion, and forgiveness. The fascinating aspect of Lennick's and Kiel's research on moral intelligence is that Lennick actually put it into practice in the field when he was the executive vice president of advice and retail distribution for American Express Financial Advisors, working with a force of 17,000 people. By putting character or "moral intelligence" first, Lennick was able to lead this team to unprecedented success.

Character lies at the heart of performance, and high-performing people in any profession are those people who, in addition to other traits, are by and large trustworthy, energetic, goal-driven, optimistic, self-reliant, inspiring to others, and compelled by a desire to prove their worth.

Character vs. Entitlement

One of the common complaints that employers give is that many of their candidates seem to have an "entitlement" complex. What they are talking about is candidates who seem to think the company owes them more than they owe the company—even before they get the job.

Here are a few examples of such complaints I have run across in the workplace.

Not too long ago, I was standing on the trading floor of one of the largest financial firms in the world, accompanied by two of my colleagues. We were discussing the firm's interest in being able to more successfully hire people fresh out of college who lacked a sense of entitlement.

"Funny you should mention that," my colleague said. "Because what we have noticed in the financial recruiting industry is this: For every 2,000 people you source as potential interview candidates for these types of jobs, you will get approximately 1,995 people who want a gold Lexus, a $175,000-a-year starting salary, every perk known to man, and a three-week vacation just to consider taking their first job. Then, you will find about five people who actually want to come in here, prove themselves, work hard, and show you what they can do."

Standing on the trading floor of that large, famous institution whose name is a household word in the financial community, surrounded by a sea of faces, with hundreds of young employees sitting shoulder to shoulder, peering at computer screens and talking on the phone in a football-field-sized space, the manager of recruiting of the firm's largest division became silent for a moment and nodded his head. Then he looked us right in the eye and spoke a few simple words. Here they are, verbatim:

"Could you, for the love of God, help us find those five people?"

Around the same time, I was talking with a training specialist for one of the branches of the armed forces, located in the Pentagon. I mentioned the same issue of entitlement that we had been discussing with the financial services firm. "Very interesting," the training specialist remarked. "We have the same problem in recruiting ourselves. As a matter of fact, it is our number-one problem—entitlement. The *what's in it for me* factor. Always putting yourself first. We are studying this intensely and we wish we knew how to screen for it, but it still eludes us. But we have been studying this problem in depth and have seen that it is creating a gigantic problem for us from boot camp on."

"What's the problem?" I asked.

"The number-one problem with entitlement, and it is a huge problem, is this," he said. "We have found that people who have this sense of entitlement you are speaking of have a complete and utter inability to work together in teams."

How Do You Know When Entitlement Is Not There?

Two of the main things we look for in order to screen for entitlement are simple things:

1. Any indication that the candidate doesn't mind putting out a little extra effort in the screening process, or isn't bothered by any of the small tasks or assessments we might require.

2. Any indication that the candidate genuinely appreciates the opportunity being offered.

Character vs. Personality

Character is different from personality. Personality may be likened to flavor—and on this earth pretty much everyone comes in a slightly different flavor. Personality, in its largest sense, is a complex description of one's individual nature, and may include measures of introversion vs. extraversion, shyness vs. friendliness, degree of baseline positive vs. negative feelings (mood), and attitude. Personality may also include the appearance of individual values, such as artistic sensibility, or the need for control. Taken to its logical conclusion (if we make *personality* synonymous with *personhood*), then personality might also include sexual orientation, favorite color, belief system, religious views, musical preferences, favorite foods, and political opinions.

Character, on the other hand (and we are taking the liberty of creating our own definition here somewhat, because a commonly agreed upon definition does not exist), is distinct from personality in that it is defined not so much by feelings and attitudes as by *actions*.

Personality tests that get at *work-related* competencies, behaviors, motivators, and attitudes can be a useful addition to the tools used in helping you and candidates decide if they are really right for the job—if they will put their hearts into it. But behavioral style preferences, aptitudes, and attitudes only describe a *potential* fit. In order to get the clearest picture of the *best* fit, candidates' potential has to be scrutinized in connection with the actions or character they have displayed in making the most of that potential *so far*. This is why the process of selecting champions has to involve both science and professional wisdom.

Selection as an Art and a Science

Jeff West is president of VantagePoint, Inc., an assessment and selection firm based in Omaha. VantagePoint has helped numerous clients build hiring and selection processes that are based on best practices and tools. Jeff believes that successful hiring is an art and a science. The science comes with the use of online assessment tools that have been validated to predict success in specific jobs and use carefully tested industry benchmarks. The art comes with applying those tools as part of a process that helps us to talk to candidates about the things that truly matter with regard to career history, accomplishments, character, and motivation.

In looking at the steps of creating a solid hiring process, these are the key questions Jeff recommends that every employer ask:

+ When it comes to making a hiring decision, do you find that you are comparing apples to oranges as a result of an inconsistent or poorly defined selection process? Do you have the right information to judge the candidate's potential for success?

+ Are you recruiting high-quality applicants?

+ Do you ensure that applicants have a clear understanding of important job requirements?

+ Are you assessing their ability (or potential) to be successful at the job?

+ Are you allowing them to self-select out of the process if the job does not fit them?

+ Are you assessing their ability to positively contribute to a work group and company success?

+ Are you maximizing applicant buy-in and participation in the process?

+ Are you maximizing supervisor and work team ownership of and commitment to good selection decisions?

The three most basic components of the hiring process that will allow you to accomplish these goals could be broken down as follows:

1. *Attract* the RIGHT candidate.

2. *Screen* strengths and weaknesses.

3. *Select* and hire the BEST.

One of Jeff's most important observations is that the selection process, if it is to be successful, must contain a "Realistic Job Preview." Only by giving candidates an in-depth view of the job can you hope to give them a fair chance to determine if they are right for the job. A Realistic Job Preview (RJP) is any part of the selection process that gives applicants a clear idea of what it will be like to work at the job if they are hired. The preview should happen early in the selection process. As West states, "The purpose of the RJP is to give the candidate[s] as much information about the job as possible so that they can make an informed decision about their suitability for the job. In order for the RJP to be successful, it must objectively outline not only the positive aspects of the job, but also the potentially negative or unique aspects of the job as well."

For example, it should include information regarding shift work, special characteristics of the job, hours, specific requirements, or a typical day on the job.

As part of the process of weaving character analysis into an overall process that includes these basic elements—candidate attraction, science-based screening, and multiphased assessment—we will turn our attention to the first item on the list: candidate attraction.

Making It Easier for Champions to Find You

One of the biggest mistakes employers and hiring managers make is not giving enough time and attention to the composition of the job descriptions and advertisements used to solicit potential candidates. This is a deadly mistake for many reasons. Here are a few of them:

Deadly Hiring Danger #1: If you don't zero in on the compelling and necessary character traits and competencies required of the job, you could end up attracting no one special—or even worse, everyone under the sun. The time and internal cost to then screen, assess, and interview hundreds of mediocre candidates will be astronomical, and the results will be endlessly confusing. You are better off narrowing the applicant pool as much as possible to begin with by letting your candidates know how demanding the job will be and what your expectations are.

Deadly Hiring Danger #2: High performers, as we have stated before, want to work for organizations they respect, and for people with whom they identify. In other words, they want to work in jobs where their heart can be in it. What are the realistic facts and messages that would lead a champion to believe he or she was joining an exemplary institution with a noble, worthy, and vital cause? What makes your organization a noble organization with which champions would be proud to be associated? Has this been put into words? Are these words present in the messages to prospective candidates?

Introductory messages to the kind of candidates you want to attract should reach the head and the heart at the same time. But how can you write such job descriptions and advertisements if you have not described what you would define as the "heart" of the job? So, starting at the beginning, the first step in finding super achievers is to write the kind of character-centered and heart-centered job descriptions that will attract them in the first place.

Here are a few critical questions you should ask yourself, before you write the job descriptions and advertisements that will attract the kind of candidates you would like to have in your pool for screening and assessment. These questions will help you construct that short list that gets to the heart of the job.

(**Note on worksheets**: In this book I made a judgment call to include the worksheets in the context of the chapter content, as opposed to putting them in an appendix where they would never be read. These worksheets are optional; if you do not want to use them, simply skip them. But I have found them useful. They describe the diagnostic format I use in working with my own clients.)

The Most Important Goal in This Job

First and foremost, I would like the person who takes this job to *prove* to me that he or she can:

_____

Accountabilities

1. What will they be accountable for?

_____

2. How will they be held accountable?

_____

3. What resources and support will they receive from their manager in order to meet the expectations to which they are being held accountable?

_____

4. How will the manager be held accountable for his or her role in supporting the efforts of the high-performing individual, once the high-performing individual is hired?

_____

Answering such questions before the hire (making sure job expectations are clearly defined in the first place, and then communicated to everyone who interviews for the job) gives you your best chance of success in narrowing your field of candidates to a select group of individuals who do not look confused when you discuss the expectations and accountabilities in the interview. In the best of all possible worlds, you want candidates who can explain in detail how they met similar expectations and accountabilities in previous jobs, how they went beyond the call of duty, and how they are prepared to do the same for you.

Insights on Character and Culture From the Marines

While I was in the process of writing this book, I had the opportunity to talk about hiring and recruiting challenges with a group of Marine Corp recruiters serving the East Coast. The recruiters made a few humorous comments about the mindset of some of the young people the Marines are dealing with these days, and I think the challenges of the Marine Corps recruiters will hit home with everyone.

"We have a name for a certain group of young people today," one of the Marines said:

We call them the "Millennials." The Millennials come after Generation X. They evolved in warp speed. Essentially, they bypassed Y and Z and went straight to the Millennial Mode. The Millennials are, for lack of a better expression, high-tech computer aficionados. They have every gadget known to man. They spend a majority of their time on the computer. They are very intelligent. And every single one of them thinks, for some reason, maybe because of what they have read in the paper, that they deserve to be the CEO of their own multi-billion-dollar international Web-based corporation by the time they are 18 years old. The idea of having to work their way up and achieve success through sweat and hard work is a foreign concept to them. Do they have a sense of entitlement? You bet. They create certain challenges in recruiting for the Marines, to put it mildly.

So what is it exactly that the Marines *are* looking for?

It seems that what the Marines are looking for is what *everyone* is looking for: a group of people who have an innate desire to prove themselves—people who do not feel that they deserve this and that, but people who would like to have the opportunity to demonstrate their worth. Such candidates, as any employer will tell you, are increasingly in the minority.

When the Marine Corp recruiters reviewed the list of "A Few Fundamental Character Traits of High-Performing People" listed in the frontispiece of this book, they indicated that these traits were very similar to the kind of character traits that the Marines are looking for in their own recruits.

But one of the most challenging aspects of their recruiting process is this: What the Marines are selling to their recruits is an *intangible*. In fact, it is what we as employers might refer to as the *great intangible*.

The Marines aren't selling *things*. They are selling a feeling. Therefore, people who are perfect for the Marines will possess certain motivations and attitudes that cause them to gravitate toward this great intangible, according to Marine recruiters.

✦ They want to work with an organization that has a worldwide reputation for honor.

✦ They want to be part of something elite.

✦ They want to have a sense of belonging among a group of individuals they respect.

✦ They want an opportunity to prove, through a trial by fire, that they are worthy of membership in this group.

✦ They want a continuing and ongoing series of difficult challenges in which to prove themselves.

✦ They want the chance to be recognized for their efforts.

✦ They want to make a difference in the world.

✦ They want others to be proud of them.

The key message for any employer who recognizes the drive associated with such dream candidates is this: You cannot possibly attract a "Marine-quality" candidate unless you have something in common with the Marines. In other words, if you want people who have such admirable character traits, motivation, and drive, then you, as an employer, have to have the traits this type of rare individual is looking for. Does your company have a reputation for honor? Is it a place such people would be proud to work? Is there a chance to make a difference in the world? Is there a chance for people to move up through the ranks if they prove themselves in a series of honorable challenges? Will they feel a sense of belonging with other great people?

These questions must be answered by every company, no matter how large or small, before anyone sets out to attract high performers.

The Character of Your Culture

Describe in as few words as possible what your company stands for and makes it an important place to be a part of:

_____

_____

In other words, what makes your organization a noble organization with which champions would be proud to be associated? Are these words present in the messages and advertisements to prospective candidates?

At Headway Corporate Resources, the company motto is "Character, Commitment, and Passion." This phrase seems to resonate powerfully with the company's team members, and also allows us to be straightforward with candidates about our culture and expectations. Your cultural motto can be the springboard for very simple questions that help you get at the issue of alignment. Using the "Character, Commitment, and Passion" motto as only one example, here are simple questions about cultural alignment that would be useful questions for any candidate:

+ Tell me about your character. What are the core character strengths you bring to the job? How have those character traits been involved in your career success so far?

+ Tell me how you demonstrated commitment to the company in your last job. What was the most difficult challenge you faced in keeping your commitments, and how did you succeed in keeping them?

+ Tell me about the professional passion that is most important to you. What drives you? Why do you feel this is a job into which you could really put your heart?

Do you see any value in asking those questions of your own candidates? What other questions concerning character, drawn from your own mission and values statements, would you ask that might elicit meaningful answers?

Here's a short list of initial questions that need to be answered in the beginning stages of mapping out the job. As we will cover in more detail later, it is good to get your top-performing employees to help you answer these types of questions.

Initial Analysis of Job accountabilities, Challenges, and Motivators

Core responsibility of the job:

_____

Forward progress that needs to be made:

_____

Qualifications: What credentials, degrees, certifications, licenses, and proven experiences of professional success must the candidate have?

_____

Core Competencies: Do you need a high level of multitasking abilities? A person who is especially structured? A person with great work organization skills? A person with great insight and emotional intelligence about others? A person who is detailed? A person who is creative and innovative? What, exactly, are those extra traits beyond experience that define the kind of goal-directed energy you need?

_____

Motivations: What aspects of your culture and the job do you think would be most motivating for the candidate? The opportunity to interact with a lot of talented people? The opportunity for rapid career advancement? A great deal of freedom? The opportunity to make significant earnings? How will the candidate be fulfilled?

_____

———

These questions should help you write the kind of job descriptions and advertisements that will help you select a higher quality pool of candidates. If you remember to tell your candidates how much you expect, and what you want them to prove to you on the job, you stand a better chance of finding and choosing those types of individuals who are actually looking for someone to whom to prove something.

Candidate–Employer Alignment

One of the components of success-oriented character is continuous forward momentum, or the perpetual desire to set and accomplish higher goals. But, of course, what the candidate needs to prove to himself or herself next should resonate with the goals of the job you may be asking him or her to fill, and you should be reasonably sure that he or she will be able to prove what *you* want him or her to prove.

One key strategy for making sure that the candidate you are about to hire for an important role will live up to all of your expectations is to carefully analyze the processes you used when you hired the last "great candidate" you thought would work out—but didn't. This initial analysis, up front, may help you with two goals:

1. Sharpening your focus on the candidate qualities that are most important to the job.

2. Identifying the parts of the process that may be most useful in getting at those traits.

As part of this strategy, you will analyze what went wrong in the hiring process of your last hire who didn't work out in a specific role, and compare it with what went right in your last best hire.

Here is a helpful series of questions you can ask as you are refining success criteria for candidates.

Analyzing Potential Gaps in Your Hiring Process:
1. What was the number-one quality I was looking for in the last candidate I thought would work out great, but didn't?

(Examples could run the gamut of benchmarking, such as proven experience in a similar job, perfect technical skills match, enthusiasm, obvious creativity, and so on.)

---

2. What pieces of evidence did I rely on to assure myself that the number-one quality I was looking for was there?

---

3. What piece of evidence contributed most strongly to my selection of the candidate I thought would work out but didn't?

---

4. What was the one quality I later discovered about the candidate that seemed to be the greatest cause of underperformance?

---

5. What is the single greatest attribute of the candidates I hired who *did* exceed my expectations?

---

6. What part of the selection process was *most* helpful to me in identifying this quality of the candidate?

    Reference checks   Interview performance

    Skills assessment   Recommendations from
                                    others
    Behavioral assessment
                                    Other evidence:
    Competency-based
      assessment

The analysis of these questions will prove helpful in examining the areas of your selection process that have been ultimately most useful in identifying top performers so far. By analyzing the components and success history of your hiring practices to date, you will be more able to see the forest for the trees in terms of simplifying and streamlining your approach to the hiring process.

The following are a few other strategies that are useful in the beginning stages of analyzing the job and creating clear expectations you can share with the candidate.

Asking Your Top Performers to Help You Analyze the Job Skills

Often, it is useful to ask your top performers to help you create the list of desirable traits that you should search for in candidates applying for identical or similar roles. After all, these top-performing employees are on the front lines. They know what skills and attributes have enabled them to win client satisfaction and loyalty.

This will also help guard against bias in the development of a success model. (As we will discuss later, additional layers of accuracy can be added by using validated competency models that can be customized for your job by a consultant who has experience in your industry.) But as one of your first steps, I highly recommend asking your top performers to help you design a simple model of success for the job. Getting their input will not only make the job easier for you, but it will also significantly strengthen your job definition model. Perhaps most important, getting this input from your current champions will help you to anticipate and be prepared for future performance needs.

This is what we will discuss in the next chapter.

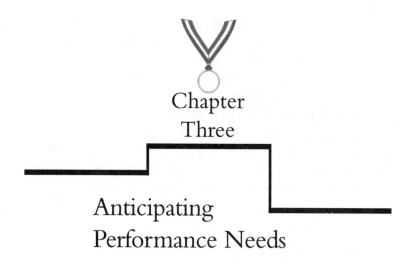

Chapter
Three

Anticipating
Performance Needs

One of the themes we will continue to explore in this book is that it is important to look at both the character traits and the competencies that are important for the job. "Competencies" is a big word, and is used in different ways by different people—it's important to talk about the differences in the language used in the marketplace.

In some definitions, human resource consultants refer to "competencies" as the entire range of skills, technical knowledge, behaviors, performance indicators, and motivations that will help predict if a candidate is best qualified for the job and will succeed in it.

For the purpose of simplicity, I find it useful to make a clear distinction up front between the skills, knowledge, and experience required for the job, and those traits that are more related to character—traits such as persistence, resilience, initiative, and a positive attitude. These are the traits that enable an individual to make the most of his or her skills, knowledge, and workplace experiences now and in the future. Typically, competencies that are character-based are also the traits that enable high performers to adapt to the stress that often accompanies difficult challenges.

Clearly, you and your colleagues have a critical role to play in helping to establish simple, bedrock benchmarks of success of the job you are trying to fill based on your own knowledge. I will refer to these as company-specific or *organizational competencies*.

Keeping It Simple

An excellent book that can be used as a guide to studying, building, and implementing competency-based interviews is Lori Davila and Louise Kursmark's *How to Choose the Right Person for the Right Job Every Time* (McGraw Hill, 2005). Mirroring themes I presented in the beginning of this book, the authors suggest keeping it simple by describing the "must-have competencies" needed for success in a particular role. The authors also suggest that one simple success match template would assign competencies to three categories:

- ✦ Technical knowledge and skills.
- ✦ Behavior-based performance skills.
- ✦ Motivations.

Competencies that predict success are different depending on the job, but you can start by asking your top performers to review a list of general ones, and then add other behavioral competencies that they think are also important.

Exercise for High-Performing Team Members

Look at this list of sample competencies, circle the three you feel are most important for your job, and explain why. Then add a few more that are not on the list and explain why they are important.

Teamwork

Sociability

Time Management

Project Management

Strategic Planning

Verbal Communication Skills

Written Communication Skills

Logical Thinking

Fact-Based Thinking

Resilience

Creativity

Innovation

Collaboration Skills

Emotional Intelligence

Teaching Skills

Learning Attitude

Risk Taking

Problem-Solving Skills

Customer Focus

Negotiation Skills

Conflict Management Skills

Crisis Management Skills

Attention to Detail

Initiative

Frustration Tolerance

Acceptance of Control and Regulations

Self-Management

Ability to Tolerate Workplace Freedom

Ambition

Listening Skills

Persistence

Persuasiveness

Ability to Handle Criticism

Insight about Others

Ability to Stay Motivated

Task-Oriented

Good Presentation Skills

Integrity

Ability to Lead and Inspire

Technical Knowledge

Ability to Deal With Change

Research Skills

♕♕♕

Employee–Driven Competency Worksheet

Three competencies the top performer(s) feel are most important from this list (if they apply):

1. Competency: _____

   Why it is important:

   _____

2. Competency: _____

   Why it is important:

   _____

3. Competency: _____

   Why it is important:

   _____

   And also, what are the competencies *not on this list* that your top performers feel are most important?

4. Competency: _____

   Why it is important:

   _____

5. Competency: _____

   Why it is important:

   _____

6. Competency: _____

   Why it is important:

   _____

(**Note:** the purpose of this exercise ties in with an observation made by Harvard psychologist Dr. Myra White in conversations we have had: Numerous companies will tell you they have found the "magic list" of competencies necessary for career success. That list does not exist. Success-based competencies are different for each job, and your analysis and observations of those competencies from your own experience are critical.)

In analyzing the cultural competencies that underlie performance, it is useful to engage current high performers who hold the same job. The goal is to help us ask candidates questions that our front-line champions know are important. Before we provide examples of how your employees can help you analyze the qualities that are part of their portrait of success, let's take a step backward and anticipate a critical moment in the interview process—what will be a moment of truth.

Anticipating the Moment of Truth

One of the most important moments in the interview is when you ask the candidate to describe his or her most significant recent accomplishments—as you attempt to discover whether those accomplishments shed light on the match between the candidate's entire skill set and the goals you need to have accomplished. Although everyone realizes that it is important to talk to candidates about their recent accomplishments, it is not always taken into consideration that questions about recent accomplishments must be broken down into at least four distinct component parts, if we are to get a clear portrait of the candidate's level of involvement in those accomplishments. Because genuine accomplishments are never achieved in the absence of challenges, it is important to anticipate such "moment of truth" questions this way:

- What is the greatest accomplishment you have made most recently in your career?
- What was the greatest challenge you faced during the process of achieving that goal?

- What was the number-one problem you had to solve in order to overcome that challenge? Were there any secondary problems you also had to solve?

- What actions did you take to address these inter-related challenges?

- What was the final result of the actions you took, and how much of the final results were related to your own individual efforts? How much of the results were linked with the contributions of your team members or others who supported you?

If you drilled down on these questions and these questions only in the interview process, many of the competencies for which you would be looking in an ideal candidate would reveal themselves—qualities such as planning and organizing, negotiation skills, delegation, detail orientation, interpersonal skills, adaptability, and so forth.

Incorporating a SPAR Analysis Before the Interview

In interviewing candidates about their accomplishments, trained behavioral interviewers often use the following model, known as the SPAR approach.

Ask the candidates to describe a particularly difficult **situation** or challenge they were able to successfully address in their previous job; get the candidate to describe the **problems** that were associated with that challenge; discuss with the candidates in detail the **actions** they took as individuals and team members to address those problems; and obtain detailed information from candidates about the **results**.

In order to create greater efficiencies in the interview process when the subject of prior accomplishments is addressed, I have found that two research techniques used in advance can be very helpful.

1. Ask the candidate to supply detailed information in advance (in writing) about previous accomplishments, and analyze the quality and timeliness of the responses as a screening device. This way, the time spent in the interview can be used for clarification of facts, not as a deposition.

2. Ask your top performers to help you analyze the key challenges they have faced and challenges they continue to face while you are in the hiring process. This will help you to better gauge the applicability of the candidate's problem-solving experiences to your own issues, and help you keep your own performance challenges top of mind as well.

To reiterate: There is seldom a need to put either the candidate or yourself on the spot by asking questions about previous accomplishments robotically with no advance preparation. Asking the candidate to submit as much of this kind of information as possible in advance, as a written document, enables him or her to provide you with more facts than you will be able to talk about or substantiate in a face-to-face interview. Poor candidates (those who are unqualified or lacking in seriousness) simply won't respond to the opportunities you present for this kind of self-assessment. They will deselect themselves. Moreover, it is difficult, if not impossible, to make up specific, fact-based, and genuine-sounding answers to the kind of questions described here, especially if the candidate is given a tight deadline, such as three to four days. In this way, you can prepare yourself for an efficient, focused, and highly structured interview. The interview time then does not become a ritualized chore, but a chance for the well-prepared interviewer (in a compact time frame) to ask a confident, relaxed, and prepared candidate to help fill in the gaps of information that need clarification—as opposed to starting from scratch with no reference points.

What makes this process even stronger is the stage at which you ask your top performers to help you set clear benchmarks of the job description that you can compare with the candidate's written self-assessments.

A Two-Tiered Approach to Deeper Job Analysis

Before interviewing candidates and asking them about their accomplishments, it may be helpful to ask several of your top performers to complete the following two-stage process that links the SPAR analysis methodology with a simple SWOT (strengths, weaknesses, opportunites, threats) analysis of your current challenges. The two-part analysis put to your top performers first could be as follows.

Combined SPAR/SWOT Analysis for Current High Performers

A. SPAR Analysis (Situation, Problems, Actions, Results)

1. As one of our high performers, what is the most difficult challenge you have faced in this job so far?

   _____

2. What is the most significant problem you encountered in addressing this challenge?

   _____

   What were the top two or three interrelated problems that contributed most to the main problem?

   a. _____
   b. _____
   c. _____

3. What are the most significant actions you took as an individual to address the main problem?

   _____

   What are the steps you took to address the related problems?

   a. _____

   b. _____

   c. _____

4. What do you feel were the top three qualities beyond skill or knowledge that helped you to achieve the results?

   a. _____

   b. _____

   c. _____

B. SWOT Analysis (Strengths, Weaknesses, Opportunities, Threats)

In light of future challenges, please give simple answers to the following questions:

1. **Our strengths.** What is the *single* greatest competitive strength we have in the marketplace today?

   _____

   What is the single greatest strength a candidate in your role needs to possess, in your opinion, in order to capitalize on this strength?

   _____

2. **Our weaknesses.** What is the greatest weakness we have as a company in the marketplace?

   _____

What is the single greatest strength an ideal candidate in your role needs to have, in your opinion, in order to help us correct this weakness?

_____

3. **Opportunities.** What is the single best opportunity you see for us to increase our marketplace share this year?

_____

What is the most important quality an ideal candidate in your position needs to possess in order to capitalize on this opportunity?

_____

4. **Threats.** What is the greatest threat facing our company from a competitive standpoint?

_____

What is the single greatest quality an ideal candidate in your role needs to possess, in your opinion, in order to help us address this threat?

_____

═══════

The goal and purpose of this exercise is to help provide a window into the most important goals and concerns shared by management and top performers in order to refine both the job description and the interview process connected with it.

This was also the overall goal of the chapter. By asking your top performers, in essence, to tell you what *they would ask of candidates* if they were doing the interviewing, you are getting the view from the trenches.

In the next chapter we will discuss an approach that is not used as often as it could be—asking candidates to tell you what they would ask if they were interviewing themselves.

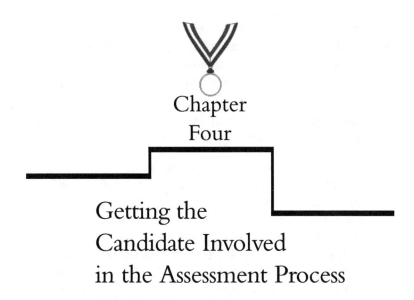

Chapter Four

Getting the Candidate Involved in the Assessment Process

One tool that is useful to both the benchmarking and assessment process is that of first asking the candidates to tell *you* what *they* think are the most important skills, attributes, and character traits for a person who would be successful in the role, after you have shared with them the parameters of the job and the key expectations.

In an initial e-mail to viable candidates, you could keep this question as simple and open-ended as possible. You don't want to prime the self-marketing pump by offering too many suggestions or examples of what you are looking for. The goal is to get at the candidate's authenticity, and to get inside the black box—separating the candidate's marketing skill from his or her genuine compatibility.

Here is an extremely simple strategy that links this chapter with the previous one. After you collect information from your top performers on questions *they* would ask the next candidate for the job, consider asking exactly the same thing of the candidate: What would *you*, as a candidate, want to know most about your skills, competencies, and qualifications, if you were the one who was interviewing?

In essence, you are involving your candidate in the assessment and benchmarking process by asking them this:

> Thank you for your interest in this position. We want to make sure that we give you the best possible opportunity to explain your competitive strengths for this role. As an initial step, please tell us what you feel are the top character strengths you bring to the job, the top skills, and the key experiences that will ensure your success in this job. Also provide a list of the most important competencies a professional in this profession needs to have. Provide as much detail as you feel is necessary to demonstrate how these traits and skills have been connected with your success in your most recent jobs, citing facts.

Again, after collecting this information from current top performers, you can both *expedite* and *add clarity to* the upcoming interview process by asking candidates to provide you in advance with a brief essay of two to three pages, describing what *they* feel are the most important skills, competencies, and character traits required of a professional in their role, and to give some evidence in writing of how those skills, competencies, and traits have been linked with their most significant accomplishments on the job recently, with a clear description of what the results were, and the process they used to obtain them.

The following is an example of such an assignment I have used in the past.

Interview Process Writing Assignment

Dear Applicant,

As part of your interview process for the position of _____, we would like you to complete a simple writing assignment. This document will help us to hold a deeper conversation with you about the strengths you would bring to this role.

Here is the assignment:

Please describe in two to three pages what you feel is your top skill, your top competency, and your top personal trait. Then explain how you have used these attributes to have success in your current job, giving specific examples of how you have met goals. Specifically, we would like to know what you feel your single greatest accomplishment on the job has been recently, the role you played in planning and executing any strategies involved, and how you may have utilized the resources of the team through any collaborative efforts. Examples are given below of the three items you should address.

Top Skill—For this point, feel free to describe all of the technical skills that enable you to excel in your profession, but try to identify, if possible, the top skill you possess that contributes most to your professional excellence.

Top Competency—For this point, please briefly discuss the most important competency you possess that allows you to persevere in the face of challenges. This special competency might be creativity, problem-solving abilities, work organization, an ability to multitask, or any other special talent or quality. It is important for us to know what you feel is your most important workplace competency beyond technical skill, and why, but feel free to share any other competencies you possess that are important as well.

Top Character Trait—For this point, please briefly describe the top personal trait that you believe has contributed most to your success in your current or last job. This could be a trait such as drive, determination, persistence, or any other trait you feel is a personal strength you bring to the job.

Make sure to give specific examples of how this personal trait and the other factors described above have helped you to meet or exceed expectations in your current or most recent job.

Using These Results

The purpose of keeping this writing request simple is to see how the candidate will respond to an open-ended task. The assignment of the exercise also enables you to compare and contrast what your current top performers perceived as the most important traits and qualities needed for the job with what the prospective candidate had to say.

As simple as it may seem, using this approach to shift part of the burden of the interview to the candidate up front allows you to accomplish many goals in a short period of time:

+ You will create greater efficiencies by allowing the candidate to "self-assess" before the interview.

+ You will be able to see how the candidate responds to the request in terms of attitude.

+ You will be able to see how the candidate responds to the request in terms of timeliness.

+ You will be able to get a better understanding of the candidate's genuine interest in the job, and a willingness to put forth "extra effort."

Moreover, this written documentation or self-assessment by the candidate submitted in advance will help you to get a much better understanding of the candidate's qualities or competencies in the following areas:

+ Attention to detail.

+ Analysis.

+ Collaboration.

+ Creativity and innovation.

+ Deadline responsiveness.

+ Follow-through.

+ Ability to deal with change.

✦ Goal-setting.

✦ Problem-solving.

✦ Organization skills.

✦ Resourcefulness.

✦ Leadership style.

✦ Negotiation skills.

✦ Resilience.

✦ Technical skills.

✦ Team-building skills.

✦ Written communication skills.

In other words, the assignment of tasks such as this helps us to find out if the candidate is entitled or not, has a good sense of dependability and follow-through, has the character traits you are looking for, takes the job seriously, and has something to prove. It's also a quick way to weed through the 300 resumes that you may have sitting on your desk.

Following is an excellent example of a character-based essay written by a former candidate who kindly gave me permission to reprint it here. Take the time to analyze it fully, and you will see how valuable such an assignment can be as part of the selection portfolio when you are trying to identify potential champions.

An Example of Excellence in a Prescreening Assignment

The following prescreening essay was written by a former candidate named Gerry St. Onge who went on to become a recruiter with Brainworks, a staffing firm based in New Jersey. Consider what you have learned about the nature of character and success once you have finished.

♛ ♛ ♛

Character Traits of Successful Salespeople
An essay by Gerry St. Onge

The Power of Intention—Goal-Setting, Determination, and Persistence

I am a firm believer in the power of intention. Setting goals and envisioning the realization of goals lines up the energy for steadfastness and insistence on reaching the goal. In your mind the goal has already been reached, it's just a matter of time and effort to realize it. With this state of mind, each task along the way is merely a means to an end. There will be successes and failures along the way—you learn from both, amplifying those things that contribute to successes and learning from and eliminating those things that have contributed to failures.

When I take on a sales challenge, I first assess the landscape of territory, company capabilities, history, etc. I then develop a set of long-term objectives (2-3 years) of what I want to accomplish. From there I can break down a set of medium- and short-term objectives, and from them develop a detailed plan of execution, knowing that I must be creative and innovative in adapting the plan as necessary along the way. This approach is very powerful in that it feeds confidence and resiliency, putting day-to-day experience (positive and negative) in the context of the big picture. It supports better judgment and decision-making along the way. When you are that determined and a bit obsessed with the end goal, hard work becomes great leverage. It's a matter of "cranking the wheel"—a function of time and effort.

This approach has contributed to my success throughout my career. I'll share one example here. At Synet, I was tasked to create new business in the northeast of the United States in the Enterprise Systems Management consulting space. Synet had a solid track record delivering tangible results for clients by transforming their customer support centers into best-in-class operations delivering best-in-class customer satisfaction. From this success, Synet targeted the wider ESM space possessing an advanced methodology and a small group of brilliant executers.

I developed long-term objectives that included establishing Synet in the northeast as the leading ESM solutions provider, establishing Synet as a partner of choice with its alliance partners in the northeast, and establishing the northeast as the most productive in sales, revenue, and profit within Synet. This was an aggressive set of goals, given that there was no existing business in the northeast. I was convinced that the market was ripe, the competition was vulnerable, and Synet brought differentiated value.

The tactical plan was heavy in cold-calling to get appointments with prospects and alliance partner regional managers. Having the end game in mind, along with the power, gave me great leverage in plowing through the many calls needed to yield the appointments necessary to kick off my sales efforts. I was able to build a $2M pipeline for Synet within 6 months, and a $4M revenue stream within 12 months.

Passion, Enthusiasm, and Optimism
In sales, as in life, if you are going after something, go all the way. Selling is fun because you create the business—you search it out, guide it, nurture it, and bring it home. The result of your work solves problems for clients and it feeds the juice of your company. You make a difference. It's very exciting. You have to believe in yourself, your company's capabilities, and the value you can deliver to your clients. You have to believe that you are helping your clients solve important business problems, and delivering business advantage to them. Your job is to win them over for their own good. They may not initially understand the value you can bring them. It's your job to show them the way; you must be tenacious to break through to demonstrate how you can help—they will thank you in the end. It's like being on a mission, and although there are bumps along the road, the mission must be accomplished for the good of your client, your company, and yourself.

Follow-Through
Ultimately, a sale requires winning and maintaining the respect and trust of the buyer. To that end, you must be very careful to set expectations, and then, preferably, exceed them. Doing what you

say you will do starts with being realistic with your promises and helping your client set realistic expectations.

Successful sales campaigns require an orchestration, coordination, and manipulation of critical variables. It's a complex project with many players, with many agendas and demands on their attention. Frequent and effective communications are critical here to maintain the buyer's attention level. It is critical to promptly confirm various things with the prospect, which represent milestones as you move through the sales process—such as requirements, commitments, and time frames—as you establish agreement on the problem and the value of your solution, and manage buyer actions culminating in deal closure. Staying close to the buyer will also best ensure that new, or currently unknown, variables can be surfaced and managed, minimizing the risk of surprises that can kill a sale.

By championing your sale, the buyer is taking on some level of risk, and you are his or her partner in the success of the endeavor. A strong sense of urgency and attention to detail demonstrates to the prospect your value as a dependable partner in realizing success and mitigating the risk of failure.

Empathy and Listening Skills

The multifaceted need of the buyer must be understood in order to craft an offer that truly meets the requirements better than the competition. Like peeling an onion, you must probe and investigate all aspects of the problem. You must know what motivates the buyer and the influencers. Sometimes the "requirements" initially described hide deeper needs, often indicating a more complex problem. Your ability to uncover what I call the "nerve source" (down to the emotional level) of the problem yields two powerful advantages. First, your understanding of the real needs, along with your solution that addresses them, offers great competitive advantage. Second, by demonstrating your ability to go beyond the stated requirements, and ideally expanding the buyers' understanding of the depth of their own problem, wins valuable consultant relationship points. The discovery process in the sales cycle has a powerful selling effect. Asking great questions and listening effectively demonstrates partner value, builds trust, and forms relationship foundations that are invaluable as you win acceptance of the solution and close the deal. I believe that leverage obtained in the discovery phase wins deals.

Problem Solving

At the end of the day we are problem solvers. For me, this is the zenith of the fun and greatest contributor to my satisfaction. We help our companies by solving the problem of increasing market share, sales, revenue, and profit. We do this by selling solutions to our clients' business problems. And in the process we have fun, find satisfaction, and make money as we continue to hone our craft.

Commitment to Continual Learning (Establish and Maintain Subject Matter Expertise and Learn From Mistakes)
Subject Matter Expertise

In any high-level sales environment, sales effectiveness requires that the salesperson be knowledgeable about the problem and solution space surrounding his or her offers. When taking on a new sales challenge, I make it a top priority to quickly build expertise such that I can engage clients in discussion about their business and probe into the potential value of my offering. This is very important. It is critical to winning trust and developing a consultative relationship with the buyer. My goal is to develop knowledge to the point at which I can engage in discovery with buyers and in short order asses their situation and identify areas for deeper discovery that suggest opportunity potential.

I signed up to be the Year 2000 Sales Exec at NCR, initially to manage a large account but also to replicate and increase business with new accounts across the country. I was to be the Year 2000 specialist. I dug in, got close to the wisest folks on the subject, quickly learned the basics, and in short order, got my arms around the space enough to identify an opportunity to expand our offering into the program management arena. I rallied the troops around it, trained NCR sales teams across the country, and personally generated significant new business for the firm. I earned a reputation as the Y2K expert among my peers and for my clients.

I knew a little bit about infrastructure monitoring software when I joined Synet. I was far from an expert on Call Centers or ESM. Once again I got close to the brilliant minds in the firm and quickly achieved a solid understanding of the problem and solution space. Within a month, I was in a position to pursue an alliance partner who was a software supplier with an aggressive message that Synet was uniquely capable to help its clients actually realize value from their software investment. This led to the opportunity to present to their sales teams, which generated leads, turning into some healthy business for me. I was also able to credibly engage with the clients at any level and discuss their ESM strategy, offering observations and insight into potential risks in their approach, leading to another stream of healthy business.

Learning from Mistakes

We never stop learning. The world is constantly changing. We can always get better. Challenges and failures provide opportunities to learn. These clichés are so true. This is one of the things that makes life so much fun, and it helps us maintain a healthy level of humility. Sometimes, when we begin to think we know it all, life has its way of reminding us about how much we still have to learn. In sales as in life, it is important to remain open to the new and to discover what can make us better in our craft and our life. It is also critical in sales and in life not to take things personally. It is hard at times, but so important to look at bumps in the road and failures as an opportunity to learn.

A Sense of Ownership and Responsibility for Results

This is a trait that I value in myself and in others. It is relatively rare in the world. It's a mindset that says I'm responsible for something and its outcomes. There are variables, some of which are out of your control, but in sales, you are the owner of your sales objectives and you are accountable for the results you are tasked to deliver. You are the manager of variables. You own the outcome. There are no excuses. If there are variables that represent risk to closure, you must act to mitigate, or if you determine that they pose significant risk, you must assess that risk and choose whether to proceed accordingly as the steward of limited resources.

Creativity and Innovation

Where there is a will, there is a way. If you are committed to realizing a goal, there are many paths to success. The commitment to "find a way" is the seed of creativity and innovation, which is critical to successful sales performance. I have been fortunate to posses some skill in this area, and it has helped me in all areas of my life.

When I began my career at NCR, I joined as a junior sales rep on the largest financial account team in the country, selling mainframe computer systems. I discovered that the client was outgrowing our operating system, which was designed for small and mid-sized banks. The OS was failing on a regular basis, becoming a major distraction for the client and an obstacle to new sales. I took on the task to fix it—I dug in, developed a relationship with our biggest critic within the client, turned her around, led NCR's development group to create a new response process for the client, and sought out and won approval to hire a third party consulting firm to provide on-site support for the client. No one gave these instructions to me—I found a way to solve the problem. I could not eliminate the bugs in our OS, but I significantly reduced the negative noise level that was hurting our sales process.

At Wang Labs I started with a territory at Citicorp that had blackballed Wang a while back due to fact that Wang had dropped a word-processing product that was well installed, and refocused resources in order to launch and support the new general-purpose and imaging processing minicomputer offering. I developed an attack plan that focused on four target offerings. I launched a recon campaign to identify suspects. I used an alliance partner's sales tracking application and launched a comprehensive campaign including sending four letters to each target before I called them to follow up—the letters culminated with an invitation to a seminar. Out of that campaign, I closed several projects, including beating out competition for an international sales automation initiative where the software I use in my campaign was deployed for the client.

Conclusion

In conclusion, I think successful selling requires a wide blend of skills, including the ability to control or manage a spectrum of variables that you do not own, but must find a way to influence. I must believe that I am providing a valuable service to my territory, prospect, and client. This feeds my passion, enthusiasm, and tenacity necessary to drive the due-diligence required to reach or exceed my objectives.

As is evident, numerous competencies were addressed in this essay, showing both a high level of self-knowledge, and great attention to detail.

Perhaps most importantly, the author is able to provide clear, logical documentation of events from the past in which the display of character just summarized was connected with *tangible results* and *tangible success*. Furthermore—and this is a big one—the examples cited in this writing sample show a *repeated pattern of success* as a result of a *habitual display* of character in the workplace.

Armed with such a document before the interview, the interviewer is in a much more informed position to study the self-reported competencies of the candidate with those that were established as critical by the department, the hiring manager, and top performers. Considering the points made by the candidate in the essay just cited, take a moment to analyze how you might apply such a tool and strategy to your own hiring process and interview preparation. Of all the competencies or attributes Mr. St. Onge mentioned, which ones are also important for the jobs you are trying to fill in your department?

Similar competencies that matter to me:

1. _____

2. _____

3. _____

If you can think of any extra ones, write them here:

Additional competencies I need:

1. _____

2. _____

3. _____

Using the information that serious, committed candidates will provide without complaint in advance as a primary research tool, interviewing the candidate becomes more of a delightful conversation than a grueling chore. You tend to prefer people who put forth effort in assessing themselves and help you to be more prepared for the interview.

And that is what the good behavioral interview is all about—informed, in-depth, carefully planned and meaningful conversations that allow the candidate to talk about the competencies, skills, and qualifications that he or she brings to the table.

Using PowerPoint Resumes

Another assignment I find useful is the assignment of the Microsoft PowerPoint resume. Resumes can be a little lifeless sometimes, and it's hard to digest hundreds of them at a time and separate the wheat from the chaff as quickly as you would like.

So, for candidates who are willing to go the extra mile, I ask them if they could turn their resume into a PowerPoint presentation and demonstrate the story of their career. I usually don't ask candidates to follow a format—I give them full creative license, because I want to see what they will do when given an open-ended creative task. I usually learn a lot about the candidate after reviewing the results of the effort. I learn about the candidate's:

✦ Enthusiasm, energy, and level of predictable future effort.

✦ Understanding of self.

✦ Creativity.

✦ Spark.

✦ Organizational skills.

✦ Marketing savvy.

✦ Self-confidence.

✦ Energy level.

✦ Attention to detail.

✦ Pride.

If the candidate were to ask for direction on the PowerPoint resume assignment, I would indicate at least the following areas as essential components, preferably in this order, unless he or she thinks of something better:

✦ Short biography.

✦ Credentials, qualifications, and certifications.

✦ Most recent jobs and duration.

✦ Greatest results achieved in last job.

✦ Core strengths.

✦ Mission in life.

✦ Key motivators.

✦ Long-term goals.

✦ Steps already achieved in attaining those goals.

✦ Chief value he or she would bring to any company.

The PowerPoint resume serves the same purpose as the essay: It gives you something more powerful than a resume. It gives you a window into the candidate's character and mind at the same time. It helps you to see the "movie" of his or her life. And it also makes an outstanding addition to the candidate's portfolio.

Ask the Candidate How He or She Would Like to Be Evaluated

One of the most powerful strategies I have discovered for helping identify top-tier candidates is so important I will put it in a box:

A Key Indicator of Accountability-Driven Candidates

Ask your candidates to tell you the three areas of performance they would like to be evaluated on and held accountable for, and why. Ask them to tell you what top three metric-driven benchmarks of success they would be holding themselves accountable for each quarter. In other words, ask candidates what they would grade themselves on if they were designing their own performance evaluation. Then, ask them how they measured up on those measurable benchmarks in the past.

By this point in the process, you have taken an exhaustive but practical and manageable look at performance indicators from the point of view of the organization and the candidate. In the next chapter, we will show you how to add another important layer of quality control through the proper use of assessment tests.

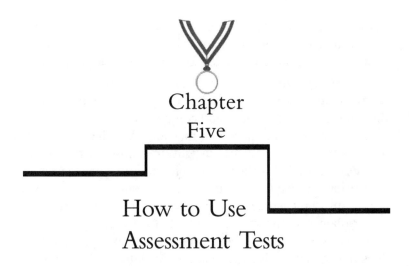

Chapter Five

How to Use Assessment Tests

The use of properly chosen assessment tests can be an invaluable aid as an additional voice in the screening and selection process. Assessment tests can present a problem, however, if hiring managers choose to focus too narrowly on one set of criteria and do not view assessment tests in the context of the full picture of the candidate's skill, experience, motivations, desire to improve, and desire to learn. Here are the guiding principles for using assessment tests: Keep it simple, keep it job-related, and keep it fair.

In my experience, it is best to work with consultants who do not approach you with a better "mousetrap" for selection, but who can explain to you and show you that their assessment and selection tools measure work-related skills and competencies that have been validated to predict success in the particular job you are trying to fill. It is usually also helpful and telling to ask for case histories from the consultant showing how any job-related assessment tests were used as part of an overall process, and how the implementation of the process led to demonstrated results in improved retention and increased productivity.

In essence, any consultant who provides you with an assessment test should be able to help you review and clarify the job expectations, goals, and competencies that are important benchmarks for success in that job. Will the assessment test help you to gain further insight into those traits, competencies, and skills? Is there a match between what the test is measuring and what you and the consultant have decided is important to measure? Can the consultant administering the test explain why the indices suggested for measurement are related to success in the specific job you are trying to fill? And does the consultant recognize and talk about the "gray areas" of assessment? Here are a few gray areas of assessment that all legitimate consultants should be able to help you with:

- ✳ Even the most rigorously tested job compatibility assessment test in the world should *only* be used as one voice in the selection process. If candidates scored low on a particular measure, could there be extenuating circumstances? How much reliance can be placed on the score?

- ✳ What other kinds of tests, reference checks, or assignments can and should be used to probe more deeply into areas of concern pointed out by the test?

- ✳ Does the consultant have any ideas about how you can use the data within the context of a larger process to give the candidate the benefit of the doubt?

- ✳ Does the test itself give meaningful feedback and built-in questions that will help you explore potential areas of concern with the candidate?

- ✳ Does the consultant administering the test seem to show a genuine respect for individual human differences that may override the importance of test findings, or does the consultant seem to be overconfident in the ability of the test?

Before you implement any assessment test, you have to explain your overall process to the consultant and say something similar to this: "Here is a list of key factors we are trying to assess in our overall process. Can you help explain to me how your assessments will help us get a better insight on job compatibility and help us make a better decision in the overall process? We want to know whether the tests are validated and job-specific. Please help us understand how your services can help our decision-making process for candidates for *this particular job* with the big picture in mind."

The best of consultants, and the most valuable of assessment tools in their process, would help you gain greater clarity on the following items:

- The hard skills and soft skills needed for the job.
- The behavioral strengths that would predict success in the job.
- The personality profile that would predict success in the job.
- The higher-order competencies that would predict success in the job.

I have said this before, but it bears repeating: Analysis and use of assessment tests results should never be used out of context with any other piece of evidence in the overall process. That is because many high-performing individuals often successfully *compensate* for any weaknesses or "low matches" found on assessment tests. Therefore, if an assessment test points out a potential job handicap, it is critical to discover, through subtle questions, whether the candidate believes the potential handicap is true, and, if so, how he or she has adapted behavior in the workplace to successfully overcome this handicap. In a subsequent section soon following, we will provide a complete checklist for monitoring the selection process, and for monitoring and guiding the use of assessment tests and assessment consultants. Before getting to that checklist, however, let us review several questions that are of critical importance in maintaining a high level of quality control in the overall process.

- ✗ Have we done everything in *our power* to make sure that the job has been clearly defined and that the candidate understands it?

- ✗ Have we done everything in our power to engage our top-performing employees in the analysis of the job and the necessary skills?

- ✗ Have we done enough research to ensure that the assessment tests we are using add insight to the process but do not overcomplicate it or lead us down the wrong path?

- ✗ If we are using assessment tests, does the consultant or person administering and analyzing the results understand our process? Will that person be able to help us use all of the information we collected to make a yes or no decision on a candidate?

In a way, you have to work backwards to determine which assessments tests and procedures (and which assessment consultants) will add the most to the process. By "working backwards" I mean that it is critical to keep the end goal in sight. Think of that final moment-of-truth interview you will have with your candidate. Will the assessment tests used bring value and clarity to that conversation between you and your candidate, or merely confuse it? In the end, someone has to say yes—not this candidate "*could be* the one" but this candidate "*is* the one." The right assessment tests, properly used, can help you and the candidate both know that yes is the right answer.

Who Will Take a Final Stand for Your Candidate and Say Yes or No?

The hiring manager and candidate have the two hardest jobs in the selection process. They are the people who ultimately have to provide the final yes and no answers that matter. Personality and competency assessment tests will often give you a "maybe" answer—the candidate *may be* a fit, but there are certain areas of concern that need to be addressed. So is the answer yes or no? Hire or not hire?

Skills tests will often give you a "maybe" answer also—there are certain skills that seem to be lacking for a best possible fit, but is it possible that those skills can be taught? Resumes will often give you a "maybe" answer—the candidate may not have the experience you are looking for, but that could be because no one has given him or her the opportunity yet to make the most of his or her true talents.

Reference checks will often give you a "maybe" answer—false positives may be created if the reference is afraid or unwilling to tell the truth, and negative biases may be created if the reference has an axe to grind.

Eight Critical Questions and Steps for Assessment–Driven Interviews: The Core Process for Hiring Champions

In the final decision-making moment, the candidate and the hiring manager will have reached a crucial juncture, in spite of potential maybes. The candidate will have to say yes to the job, and the hiring manager will have to say yes to the candidate. In order to make sure that yes is the best answer for both parties, the hiring manager will have to ask these questions in some way, though the language will be personalized:

1. We feel that we have done our best to fully explain the demands and expectations of the job, and the qualifications required. Do you feel that you fully understand the job as we have described it? Do we need to do anything else to clarify our expectations?

2. If you do understand the job, the expectations, and the qualifications, could you please explain it back to me so that I know beyond a shadow of a doubt that we have the same understanding?

3. Are you fully confident that you have the skills to succeed in this role? If not, what makes you think you can learn them quickly enough? Please do not allow us to set you up for failure. If you cannot convince me that you are 100 percent confident that you will succeed, do not let us offer you the job.

4. We have done our best, using assessments as necessary, to determine the type of behaviors, personality traits, and competencies that may be most predictive of success in this job. We have shared a few potential concerns from these assessments. Do you feel they should be concerns for us? If not, explain why you feel the assessments were off-base, or why they should not be of concern to us.

5. We need to hire people who rigorously assess their own performance day by day. People who want to be accountable to themselves. So, if you were to draft your own performance appraisal, what is it that you would like to be measured on, and why?

6. When you think about the type of work environment that will make you happy, and give you a sense of continuous fulfillment and the opportunity for growth, have we described it? If so, tell me why. If there are any areas of concern that you need us to clarify with regard to your opportunities for growth and fulfillment, let's talk about that now.

7. What makes you most optimistic about your chances of success here? What are the differences in the job or the environment that makes this a better fit than other jobs you have had or looked at?

8. This is too important of a life decision for either of us to make a hasty decision. So, I want you to take three days. I want you to consider all of the reasons you want this job, and also to consider any situation that could cause you to fail. Within three days, please send me an e-mail explaining why you are confident in us, and why we should be confident in you.

The Wrong Candidates Will Not Make It Through the Process

No person who is not a high-potential candidate (and who fully understands and wants the job) could possibly fake answers to such questions by reading any book, or attending any interviewing skills seminar.

Few people who have not adequately self-assessed their own fit for the job will make it through those questions, or have a clear and confident answer for you three days later.

The proper role of assessment tests is to help you hold the conversation cited previously, with more clarity. The best and brightest assessment experts and consultants I know understand what the end goal is, and understand that assessment tools help add clarity to the process.

Before you decide to use an assessment test, it is important to share all of the important data points of selection with your assessment consultant, and to see what evidence he or she can provide to help you add value to the process. Here is a checklist that covers many of the important points for consideration. This list is not designed to score the candidate, but to score the process, and to judge how closely you have come to being able to make a yes or no decision with the *candidate's input and agreement.*

The purpose of the checklist will be to review how many yes's, no's, and maybe's there are on the page. In the best of all possible worlds, your goal is to have as many yes's as possible, if you are to be certain that no stone has been left unturned in your hiring process. However, if there are no's and maybe's on your list, there are numerous questions that you need to ask yourself before making a final decision on any candidate.

The lower the score, or the more maybe's you have, the more the process may need to be examined and tweaked. Higher scores (more yes's) means that you have left fewer stones unturned in your analysis of the job, the qualifications, and the fit. You have performed a high degree of due diligence to assure yourself that the candidate is qualified and the job match is there. But as for the final yes or no answer? That is between you and candidate, after addressing the eight critical points discussed earlier. The following checklist will simply put you in a better position to address the eight critical points in the final interview with the candidate.

The items in bold refer to the areas that a qualified assessment expert could help you clarify—as long the tools are **industry-specific** and **validated**.

―――――

Sample Checklist for a Fair and Complete Selection Process

Candidate: _____

0=No   1=Yes   ?= More Information Needed (Maybe)

Job description: _____

―――――――――――――――――――――――――

<u>Score</u>

1. Does the candidate understand the job description? _____

2. Does the candidate understand what you do and what makes you different as a company? _____

   Key expectations communicated in advertisement:

   _____

   _____

3. Does the candidate understand the expectations? _____

   Top three goals of the job:

   a. _____

   b. _____

   c. _____

4. Does the candidate understand the goals? _____

5. Has the candidate achieved similar goals in the past? _____

   Top three skills desired:

   a. _____

   b. _____

   c. _____

6. Does the resume reflect these skills? _____

7. Have these skills been exhibited so far in the candidate's response to the selection process? _____

8. **Has an assessment test been given on job-specific skills, and is the candidate qualified?** _____

9. Do the skills that can be taught make up for deficiencies? _____

10. Does the candidate express a strong desire to learn those skills? _____

   Three top **behaviors** desired (e.g., initiative, follow-through):

   a. _____

   b. _____

   c. _____

11. Have those traits been exhibited so far in the candidate's response to the selection process in terms of actions displayed? _____

12. Did the interview indicate that the person displayed those traits in the last job? _____

13. Has a validated, job-specific test been given on desired behaviors, and is the candidate a match? _____

   Three top competencies desired (e.g., organizational skills, time management):

   a. _____

   b. _____

   c. _____

14. Have those traits been exhibited so far in the candidate's response to the selection process? _____

15. Did the interview indicate the person displayed those competencies in the last job? _____

16. Has a validated, job-specific test been given on desired competencies, and is the candidate a match? _____

Three top personality traits desired: (e.g., positive outlook, sociability):

a. _____

b. _____

c. _____

17. Have those traits been exhibited so far in the candidate's response to the selection process? _____

18. Did the interview indicate that the person displayed those traits in the last job? _____

19. Has a validated, job-specific test been given on desired personality traits, and is the candidate a match? _____

Three top motivations desired (e.g., financial motivation, desire for recognition):

a. _____

b. _____

c. _____

20. Have those traits been exhibited so far in the candidate's response to the selection process? _____

21. Did the interview indicate that the person displayed those traits in the last job? _____

22. Has a validated, job-specific test been given on desired motivators, and is the candidate a match? _____

23. Was the resume accurate, and did the skills and experiences relate? _____

24. Did reference checks verify the resume? _____

25. Did the candidate ask thorough and clarifying questions about the job? _____

26. Has the candidate explained the areas he or she would like to be evaluated in once performance reviews roll around? _____

27. Is the candidate able to explain in detail results of the last performance review in his or her last job? _____

28. Do the reference checks confirm this information? _____

29. As opposed to looking for a partial fit, does the candidate really want to do this job?

30. Was the candidate able to articulate his or her core strengths? _____

31. Did the candidate have an understanding of areas for improvement, and an action plan? _____

32. Does your gut instinct about the candidate's potential and character override any potential weaknesses? _____

33. Is the salary acceptable to the candidate? _____

34. Is the travel acceptable to the candidate? _____

35. Are the hours acceptable to the candidate? _____

═══════

If you feel that you have given as much attention as you can or is necessary to securing yes answers for the preceding items, then you have done a great deal to help ensure that the candidate knows you, and that you know the candidate.

Job-specific assessments (especially those that are competency-based) can help you clarify many of these points, such as the behavioral skills, personality profiles, and competencies that have been proven to be useful as part of the selection process. There are two ways to get at competency benchmarking—do it yourself, or use a validated instrument. I think both are useful as data points, and so I will explain them in order.

Two Ways to Get a Competency Assessment: Internal Assessment and Validated Assessment

Developing internal competency outlines is a worthwhile exercise, simply because it gets the company thinking about competencies—for many companies, that act in and of itself usually creates forward momentum. In an earlier chapter, we gave exercises that showed how you could use feedback from top performers and other internal contributors to create a simple and practical success model built around competencies. The analysis of competencies in-house is a key step forward in creating competency-driven organizations when companies use the information to help hold deeper conversations with candidates. Such an in-house analysis of competency can help you better identify the expectations and success predictors of the job—using your own knowledge, asking top performers to help you identify those traits, and then seeking information from the candidates themselves to see what *they* think the success predictors are. This allows you to see how much consistency and alignment there is between what *you* think, what your *team member*s think, and what the *candidate* thinks.

Following is an example of a worksheet you can use to as a template to help study the applicability of standard competencies in your environment. Using this as a guide, you can replace any items that do not apply with competencies that emerged from your own internal analysis, as described in previous chapters.

Measurable Traits That Make Sense to Measure

Take a moment to study the following scale. (The scale describes a few competencies that can be measured by validated, industry-specific selection tools.) Think of your own job, or the job of a person with whom you may work. Make two photocopies of the survey page, and study the survey from two vantage points:

1. While you are contemplating your own job, the job of an employee or colleague, or a job you are seeking to fill, try to give a realistic score for the degree of performance one would need to exhibit to do that job well. Again, be realistic; everything can't be a 10. For some jobs you will not need or even want all of the traits to a high degree. That's the point—most jobs require a different set of competencies.

2. Next, take the test again as if you were evaluating yourself, your colleague, or a recent candidate whose background you studied carefully after asking pertinent questions of people who have seen them in action before. Is there a discrepancy or gap?

Examples of Work-Related Competencies and Traits

Please use a 1 to 10 scale when grading the requirements of the job in each of the following areas. The highest score is 10, and 1 is the lowest. Again, be realistic. Not every item can be (or should be) a 10. Different jobs require different competencies. The scores you give indicate what qualities the candidate would bring to the job in the best of all possible worlds.

____	Work pace	____	Need for recognition
____	Self reliance	____	Detail orientation
____	Work organization	____	Assertiveness
____	Multitasking	____	Positive about people
____	Follow-through	____	Insight
____	Acceptance of control	____	Optimism
____	Frustration tolerance	____	Criticism tolerance
____	Need for freedom	____	Self control
____	Desire to conform		

Now that you (and perhaps a few others on your recruiting team) have realistically scored such a sheet and created a benchmark for a particular job, you may want to ask a candidate in an interview to honestly give an appraisal for themselves on the same points. This kind of assessment will not give you validated results the way an actual predictive assessment can, and should not be used as a selection device to make judgment calls on candidates, but it could give you a format for asking deeper questions of the candidate, while helping to explain what a "good fit" for the job really means from your point of view. Studying this scale (as an example only) will also help guide you in your discussions with assessment consultants as you work together to create benchmarks for customized success models built on industry templates.

Also, as you study and create benchmark tools for the particular job you are seeking to define, you can add other factors that you know are important, and delete the ones that are not. For example, you might add the following to your list:

- ✦ Collaboration skills.
- ✦ Creativity.
- ✦ Problem-solving skills.

The point is, the development and use of such benchmark sheets help you and your team to better analyze the real requirements of the job, and to help you better explain your expectations to candidates.

Becoming "Competency-Conscious"

There is another good use of benchmark sheets that describe the work-related qualities you are looking for in candidates: They provide excellent questions for reference checks. In other words, when you research an individual's record of performance in the workplace using reference checks that stay focused on job-specific measurements, such as the ones mentioned here, you have something more tangible and more appropriate to discuss than "what can you tell me about this person?"

One of the elements that is not covered by competency models built in-house, however, is industry data on the competencies and skills of top performers in similar jobs. That is why the most thorough selection and screening process will also include a review of industry-benchmarked competencies, and the use of assessment that can help identify such competencies in the top candidates.

Using Validated Selection Tools With a Competency Focus

Using validated, *industry-specific* competency models as part of the selection process will help you to ascertain whether you may have overlooked important skills, behaviors, and competencies that are relevant to the job in your own initial analysis.

These assessments and selection tools, such as the ones offered by ASSESS Systems of Dallas, are extremely helpful (and often essential) in providing additional insight on the traits that may be most important to look for in candidates, and the ones that may not be as critical. This provides an extra layer of due diligence in helping to insure that good potential candidates are not weeded out of the process because of false assumptions about necessary job skills.

As opposed to measuring vague or tangential concepts that someone imagined might be related to success on the job, ASSESS Systems's instruments examine, among other issues, 24 scales based on 350 items derived from the Guilford-Zimmerman Temperament Survey, which incorporates about 50 years' worth of data and ongoing research into the traits that have been *proven* to correlate with performance in the workplace.

Utilizing this model, ASSESS Systems builds scientifically valid "competency models" for specific jobs, and its assessments (which genuinely use competency data, unlike some assessments on the market, which use generic and oversimplified behavioral models) examine job competency models from a precise, job-specific point of view.

A good example of this can be seen in the results of the SalesMax test developed by ASSESS Systems, which has been shown to predict performance in earnings in various types of sales jobs.

Sales Force Analysis Using Validated Tests

In brief, validation studies conducted on the usefulness of the SalesMax assessment shows that knowledge of the sales process and personal motivators do not strongly correlate with earnings in top sales professionals. Here are the traits that were found to be associated with higher earnings:

- ✦ Energy Level.
- ✦ Follow-through.
- ✦ Optimism.
- ✦ Resilience.
- ✦ Assertiveness.
- ✦ Social Skills.
- ✦ Expressiveness.
- ✦ Serious-mindedness.

These are among the traits that are often important to measure for professionals in other occupations as well. It is extremely interesting to me that skill, knowledge, and experience did not correlate with earnings in sales professionals, but that these traits did. From this study alone, we can see that there are certain fundamental, core traits of a person's character, attitude, and approach to the job that may be far more important to consider than skill.

Once the core traits for success in a job are benchmarked, and supported by validated assessments, the interviewer is much better prepared to ask the questions that will reveal the behaviors supporting such traits. The interviewer will not only be better prepared to discuss these core traits with the candidate, but the interviewer will also be able to have more meaningful conversations with references.

Limitations of Assessment Tests

Instead of abandoning judgment and giving tests a godlike status, those in charge of hiring must use common sense and realize that it is logical to use job-screening processes and tools as conversation pieces *only* as they are seeking to help job candidates explain their aspirations and the track of diligence they may have documented in pursuing their aspiration so far.

According to leading employment lawyers, the following questions should always be asked when considering the use of any employment screening test:

- What is the purpose of the test?
- What function does it serve?
- What job characteristics am I looking for?
- How does the test serve that purpose?
- How widely is that test used in my industry?
- Is the test outdated, or has it been updated?
- How would I feel if I, or a family member, were subject to this test?
- Are there questions that seem particularly sensitive or raise concerns about an individual's mental state?

Character-Based Reference Checks

In this context of creating job-related interview questions, questions such as the ones on the following list can certainly be used as a reference point in thinking about, talking about, or asking questions about an individual's track record in a previous job or jobs:

- Does the individual have a track record of honesty?
- Does the individual have a track record of reliability?
- Does the individual have a track record of persistence?
- Does the candidate demonstrate an ability to work with others and be part of a team?
- Does the candidate have a track record of a strong work ethic?
- Does the candidate have a track record of following up on matters of importance?

Clearly, as an employer, you have a right to consider whether people you are about to hire have demonstrated these or similar traits in previous jobs (if these traits are important to you), and you have the right to seek out such information in reference checks, if the reference is willing to share his or her thoughts on these job-performance–related issues.

For some jobs, you may assert that persistence, or another factor listed, is not so important to you. And that is fine. But we highly recommend that you make a list of the character traits that *are* important to you for specific jobs. Again, a character trait, by our working definition, is a trait that can be documented by an *observable action pattern of behavior throughout time*.

Additional Advantages of Using Validated Competency Models

In recent years, many companies have used the concepts of competencies and competency models to define the broad behavioral capabilities necessary to achieve the behavioral objectives that will guide the activities of people in the organization. Others have used concepts such as success factors or human capital strategies to describe critical abilities and attributes desired in employees to give the organization a workforce that will be able to achieve strategic goals.

These concepts and others focus human resource processes on the most important capabilities, and provide a global framework for defining desired behaviors and the knowledge, skills, and other attributes necessary for achieving these behavioral goals. If they are well developed, competency models will capture not only the business strategy, but also the critical elements of the corporate culture and values.

The biggest obstacle in the popularization of competency models is efficiency, both in the development and in the implementation of models. Often, companies avoid undertaking competency modeling because they perceive the effort required to be too great: "It will take too many people, too much time, and too much money to develop." The second major obstacle occurs at implementation. Finding a way to quickly and efficiently link selection tools (such as assessments and interviews) or development tools (assessment, 360 feedback, developmental resources, and so on) to competency models is a challenge that many organizations face.

The value of online assessment testing is that it provides a wide array of pre-employment tests and development assessments for current employees. These tests are designed to be used in an integrated selection process; each includes an interview protocol and follow-up interview probes based on test results. Although each test measures characteristics important to a specific job type, all have at their core the prediction of productivity, cooperative work behaviors, and integrity.

It is important to make sure that the tests you use are developed by organizational psychologists, validated for specific jobs and industries, and predictive of job success. As explained by the industrial psychologists we work with, processes incorporating the right assessment tests can help companies create a model for strategic human resources and accomplish the following goals more effectively.

* Understand what the company's customers want and need.

* Do the right things to consistently meet or exceed customer expectations.

* Focus on the most important things to achieve these expectations.

* Incorporate all of this into a well-defined strategy.

People in prosperous companies use this strategy to guide:

+ How they spend money.

+ Which products and services they offer.

+ How they organize themselves.

+ How they staff their organization.

+ How they define what their people should do.

+ How they translate strategy into human requirements.

+ How they define the best behavior to achieve strategic goals.

+ How they specify the desired skills, abilities, and personal attributes for people at all levels in the organization.

Good competency models help to guide these HR processes:

+ Performance evaluation.

+ Compensation.

+ Training and development.

+ Recruitment and selection.

+ Talent management/succession planning.

Strategic Tools for Talent Management

Leading companies are also utilizing the following additional services and tools provided by industry-validated competency models.

1. **Validated executive and managerial assessment development tools**, delivered securely online. These tools are specific for many industries (such as finance, insurance, healthcare, and aerospace), and help assess whether executives possess the core competencies and skills needed for success in their jobs. The assessments also help determine whether

the executives possess the traits necessary for mentoring and educating those they must supervise.

2. **Integrated online courseware** for helping executives improve the competencies necessary for success in their roles, including the mentoring, training, and management of others.

3. **Validated executive and management selection tools** (delivered securely online) that help predict executives and managers who will be most successful in a wide range of positions across many industries. The competencies assessed are specific to executive and management roles within those industries.

4. **Talent management and performance management scorecards**, and other metric-driven tools, linked with the validated assessment and development tools described previously. These tools enable organizations to clearly track and study the link between improved selection and team development processes, as well as outcome measures for success established by the organization.

5. **State-of-the art employee surveys and 360s**, to enable a reliable and scientifically valid study of team members' perceptions regarding management effectiveness, the meeting of goals and expectations, and many other issues affecting performance management. These 360s and employee surveys can also be linked with the job-specific competencies studied by selection and development tools to get an even broader picture of an organization's performance potential and areas that may need improvement.

6. **Validated and job-specific selection tools for front line workers** such as administrators, sales and sales support personnel, call center professionals, healthcare workers, and other employees in specific support jobs across most industries.

As stated at the beginning of the chapter, it is important to ask any assessment consultant working with you to help explain how the use of these tools can be incorporated into the overall process, using case histories wherever possible. Following is a case study from ASSESS Systems and my partners at VantagePoint, Inc., showing how the use of assessment tests as an overall selection improvement process was able to significantly affect earnings.

♛ ♛ ♛

Development of a Successful Hiring Model at a Major Call Center: Using Assessments as Part of a Process

The Issue

A large international call center organization with locations in more than 32 countries needed a solution to its hiring challenges. The company had a high turnover rate, and had implemented several measures it hoped would alleviate the problem. After reviewing and enhancing its compensation rate, creating a hands-on realistic job preview, and redesigning its training program, the company was still concerned about the rate of turnover.

Diagnosis

It was determined that the company was missing the last critical piece to its process. The company needed a pre-employment testing tool that would help identify those individuals who had a productive attitude, were good at persuasion and diplomacy, and liked to work in a structured environment where performance is closely monitored.

Actions

A complete job analysis was conducted, identifying those characteristics important for success, and a large group of call-center agents were tested using a custom-developed test battery. Performance ratings were analyzed—the results were statistically significant. The newly developed survey was added to the selection process and launched in all locations, providing hiring consistency throughout all sites and eliminating any cultural bias.

Result

Lower turnover and increased productivity were evident in a short period of time. Within four years, turnover had significantly dropped from double digits to 4 percent. Equally importantly, productivity also improved. Booked revenue increased significantly above the 12 percent annual increase goal to no less than 20 percent on a consistent basis each year.

The purpose of presenting the case history was to reiterate a key point we made earlier: before implementing assessment tests, make sure the consultant who is advising you can provide clear case histories showing how the assessments were used as part of a larger process, and how they helped to achieve documented results.

So far in the book we have focused on tools and processes for helping to identify top performers and improve the process for selecting them. In the next chapter, we will begin to focus more intensely on the "spirit" of excellence, showing how and why high-performing individuals are those individuals who are true to themselves, and who have carried this authenticity into most of the career decisions they have made.

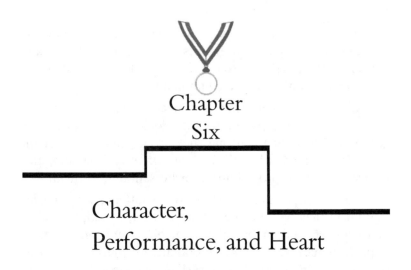

Chapter
Six

Character,
Performance, and Heart

Great coaches and hiring managers often refer to character as "heart."

Contemplating the importance of heart, many readers may be reminded of scenes from a number of great films or stories in which the importance of heart is the greatest lesson learned. From the dawn of history, people have been moved by stories of courage that depict the indomitable nature of the human spirit. All high-performing individuals, first and foremost, seem to possess that indomitable spirit.

It is our observation that high-performing individuals, by and large, are just great people, period. In many ways they symbolize the optimism, strength, self-reliance, and hope that are always the hallmark traits of admirable people.

In addition, high-performing individuals only have one competitor—themselves. They're never competing against colleagues, or anyone else. There is a bar inside their heads that's constantly moving up, and they will always be slightly dissatisfied by yesterday's achievements. The only thing that really matters to them is their next big victory, which has to be bigger than the last, if it's going to count at all.

All great managers know this, because when they are describing the kind of people they are looking for, they always get around to telling you that they are looking for a person who's still hungry, who still has that drive and passion, and who still wants to prove himself or herself all over again.

Another important trait is a positive outlook, or optimism. Optimism may well be the umbrella trait, or "alpha trait," that supports and enables the other nine fundamental traits of performance we have listed. Looking for signs of optimism (which is strongly related to resilience) is such an important part of the interview process and the makeup of high-performing individuals, that we will spend a few moments talking about it.

The Holy Grail of Excellence

People often ask if there is a "master trait" for predicting excellence in high achievers. Some have said that the search for the greatest single trait of excellence is as futile as the search for the Holy Grail. Actually, it may not be that elusive—if you examine all of the leading research on the personality traits or character traits of the highest-grossing salespeople (who serve as an excellent research population for studying high performers in general). Studying the traits of top-grossing salespeople as they have been investigated throughout the past 40 years or so, I believe you will find that one trait is common to all: *balanced optimism*.

All other predictable traits appearing in great salespeople are dependent on the resilient energy and commitment that optimism provides. Great salespeople (those who make the most money) are able to weather the brutal discouragements that come in the sales life, perhaps because their brains are wired differently. Drawing on brain-wave research, we can say (in layman's terms) that people with a high degree of "positive affect" or "optimism" have more electricity flowing through the areas of the brain that control approach-related or "proactive" style behavior. Partly because of this excess energy in specific areas of the frontal brain, these relentlessly proactive optimists may be predisposed to viewing most events in a positive light, even in situations in which other people may see only tragedy or defeat.

The Case for Balanced Optimism

Optimism alone does not a high achiever make. Many high achievers (especially those in business) also have a cautionary, analytical side that combines good judgment with that optimism, and this combination of aggression and optimism, along with good judgment or solid analytical reasoning, is actually rare.

During the interview process, make sure to ask the candidate about risks he or she has taken, what the decision-making process for taking those risks was, and what the results were. Optimists take risks, but not ill-informed risks.

Although it has been said many times by many people, positive outlook, or optimism, may be one of the traits that underlies every other trait, including the 10 fundamental ones we cite as principles.

Norman Vincent Peale, for example, made a legendary career out of promoting and describing one utter truth: that the mere act of simply trying to think positive thoughts, even in negative situations, sets into motion a domino effect of success-patterned behavior. In other words, people who think positively are more inclined to take chances, follow up, and be persistent, which are other core traits of character-based success.

A host of other writers, from Dale Carnegie (*How to Win Friends and Influence People*) to Anthony Robbins (*Unlimited Power: The New Science of Personal Achievement*), and virtually every other self-help guru known to man, has preached the proposition that if you choose to think positive thoughts, even in the face of setbacks, almost every other goal in your life will *naturally* and *eventually* fall into place.

So many examples of this truth abound that we can almost cite optimism and persistence as natural laws—make the conscious and deliberate decision to remain optimistic in spite of setbacks, and then persist, and you will eventually become successful. (Of course, we are speaking of balanced, rational optimism, as discussed earlier. People who are balanced optimists are level-headed and do not gamble foolishly. That is, there is a big difference between taking a risk on a musical career—if you honestly believe in your talent and have enough resources to responsibly pursue your dream—and throwing away your child's college fund on the slot machines in Vegas. The first is an example of balanced optimism, the second is an example of either foolishness or an addiction.)

In many ways, the psychological effects described in such theories as Neural Linguistic Programming are in fact common sense, in a way—the way you choose to speak to yourself does seem to have a profound effect on your abilities. If you tell yourself that you are a failure, for example, just because you have not succeeded in one stage of your endeavors, you are not likely to approach the all-important tasks of follow-up and persistence with joyful, optimistic energy—and at that point, you become a self-fulfilling prophecy, a victim of your negative self-speak.

Because the world has so many self-help gurus these days, the discussion of positive thinking as the ultimate key to success often runs the risk of being ignored, or dismissed as psychobabble. However, a series of in-depth studies by such notable psychologists as Dr. Martin Seligman demonstrate that this age-old truth is just as profound today as it was 10,000 years ago.

The Scientifically Validated Power of Optimism

As we discussed earlier, one of the 10 fundamental character traits of high-performing individuals is positive attitude or optimism. In this book we will provide a thorough explanation of how the traits of optimism and friendliness should be handled as sought-after traits or indicators, given the law. In fairness, as we said, it is not reasonable to suggest that all jobs should require or can require an optimistic attitude or mood. But on a certain level of common sense, one may gather that in certain jobs it helps to be friendly to the customer and have some sense of positive outlook about life.

In the next section we will discuss why it is appropriate to put optimism or positive thinking on the list when considering the attributes of many (although not all) high-performing individuals.

Optimism as a Source of Happiness

In a compelling couple of books titled *Authentic Happiness* and *Learned Optimism*, past president of the American Psychological Association Dr. Martin Seligman makes a joyful argument that psychology should be more focused on nurturing the noble and happy tendencies in people, as opposed to looking for dysfunctions that can be treated.

In addition to being a popular author, Seligman is also a coauthor with Christopher Peterson on the academic masterpiece *Character Strengths and Virtues* (Oxford University Press, American Psychological Association, 2004). This book defies synopsis—it is a brilliant, exhaustively researched, and meticulously annotated and footnoted research compendium of character strengths that have a measurable, scientific quality to them (as opposed to a moral quality), and can be reasonably tied to success in life. The umbrella traits are: wisdom and knowledge, courage, humanity, justice, temperance, and transcendence. Each trait is broken down into components of sub-traits that bolster the main trait. (For example, the sub traits of transcendence are appreciation of beauty and excellence, gratitude, hope, humor, and spirituality.) It's easy to see how this phenomenal effort in character research applies to you. Simply go to *www.authentichappiness.sas.upenn.edu* to take or review the authentic happiness survey. You will get an instant 10-page report on your own signature strengths. We will discuss more of Seligman's groundbreaking work in subsequent chapters, but for the moment it may suffice to briefly describe one of his most provocative themes.

According to Seligman, one's level of optimism or pessimism does not have to stay forever the way it is. In Seligman's model, we can become happier in time if we learn that, to a certain extent, optimism is a *choice*. That is, we can choose to view the events in our lives with more of a positive slant, should we choose to do so. Granted, learning how to have a more positive outlook on events that may appear to us as mostly negative now doesn't happen overnight, Seligman explains, but can be done with persistence, dedication, and practice. And by practicing the art of choosing optimism, or a positive outlook, we can gradually learn to be happier. (Here is another fine example, as you may have already noted, of the way our 10 fundamental character traits of high-performing people are interrelated. In this case, the daily practice of using one positive character trait, persistence or *dedication*, makes it possible to increase optimism. And then the increased optimism creates the energy that enables greater levels of persistence, which further increases optimism, in a spiraling effect. Future research may indeed demonstrate that it is this spiraling effect of certain character traits reinforcing one another through practice that has the most profound effect on separating high achievers from those who reach lower levels of achievement.)

Optimism is an area that has been studied from many different angles. I was involved in some of those studies as a graduate student, where I helped to conduct studies on brain waves and personality at the Mind/Body Medical Institute of Harvard Medical School, while pursuing a master of liberal arts degree in psychology. We found that there is a biological marker for optimism, or "positive affect," in the amount of electrical current flowing through certain regions of the frontal brain. These biological differences, moreover, have been shown to be present from birth. In other words, some people seem to possess a biological predisposition for optimism, which may mean it may be easier for them to have a positive outlook than it is for others. However, the wild card question is whether traits such as optimism may be malleable, and can be changed in time if an individual makes a courageous effort to change his or her perceptions. Seligman is one of those learned professionals who believes that such core traits can be changed by the personal will to be happier, and I believe that he is probably right, based on the substantial evidence he provides.

Another key component of happiness, which Seligman addresses in *Authentic Happiness,* is authenticity. By this, Seligman essentially means that it is necessary to follow our own dreams and the inclinations of our hearts—our true, authentic desires—as opposed to leading the lives we think we ought to lead, whether we are trying to please our parents, appease a spouse, or keep up with the Joneses. Living someone else's dreams leads to misery, Seligman suggests, but living our own dreams leads to joy.

Other Ideas on the Traits of Peak Performers

If we accept the idea, as Seligman suggests, that optimism is to a certain extent a choice, then it is also within reason to propose that optimism gives high-performing people the green light, so to speak, to take risks, hope for the best, and practice the art of *faith*.

Let me explain what I mean by this.

If you look at the work other researchers have done on the traits of high-performing individuals, and you analyze those traits, it becomes apparent that much of what you see amounts to constant preparation and practice—what one might call **practicing for success**. In other words, high-performing individuals, according to the research of others who have studied them, seem to have a laundry list of things they do during the day, which they practice, in much the same way a musician practices scales. And what they get from all of this practice is a sense of accomplishment—even if they hit a sour note every once and a while. Low-performing individuals, to extend the example, would hit a sour note while practicing scales and say, "That sounded horrible. I have no talen. I might as well give up." The high-performing individual will say, "Sure, it sounded horrible, but that's because I haven't practiced enough. So let's go over those scales one more time."

A popular parable from history often cited as a schoolbook example of character and persistence is the story of Abraham Lincoln, who failed at many businesses and jobs before he became a successful politician and later president of the United States. When you look at people such Abraham Lincoln, who personify persistence and resilience, you actually see people who do not view failures as failures—in their minds they are merely practicing for success, and no matter how many sour notes they hit, or how much they are criticized by others, they will keep on practicing until they get it right.

One well-regarded scholar on the traits of high-performing individuals is Charles Garfield, who published a book entitled *Peak Performers* (Harper Paperbacks, 1986). In that book, Garfield spelled out what he found through his own research to be the key traits of high-performing individuals. Using some of his main findings as points of inspiration, I have written a list of practice points that high-performing individuals give to themselves, as a job and matter of *choice*. The key word in the sentences following is the word *will*. High performers are largely successful because they *will* themselves to be successful. Here are some of the points high-performing individuals practice during the day.

The Fundamental Principles of the Will to Succeed

✖ I will spend some time every day plotting a strategy for my success.

✖ I will set high goals for myself and raise my own bar. Even if I don't immediately achieve these goals, I will keep trying.

✖ I will maintain a high degree of confidence and self-esteem for myself, no matter what anyone else says about me.

✖ I will love myself and I will love others.

✖ I will reward myself for being responsible by proudly taking credit for my best ideas.

✖ I will mentally rehearse important events in my mind before they happen and picture myself winning.

✖ I will learn from my mistakes, but I will hold no regrets for anything I have done wrong.

✖ I will not waste any of my time, but will make the most of every day.

✖ I will not worry if other people don't see me as successful, but will continue to strive, knowing that persistence always pays off—each and every time, without fail.

✖ I will continue to be as innovative as I can. If one method fails, I will try another.

✖ I will not be afraid to ask people to help me, because I realize that nothing great is ever accomplished without the help of others.

✖ I will make a conscious choice to feel good about my work environment.

* I will continue to believe, no matter what, that I can make a valuable contribution by the work that I do.

* I will continue to believe that the work I do will help make the world a better place or help people in some way.

* I will strike quickly and without hesitation when I see an opportunity that will benefit me and will not foolishly risk my financial resources.

* I will imagine in advance the worst that could happen with my plans, and I will create a strategy in advance to deal with those events if they come up.

* I will spend some quiet time with myself each week taking an inventory of my blessings and victories for the week, and I will write them down.

The key takeaway from this list, for managers, is that successful or high-performing individuals usually have a record of practicing such principles on a daily basis, and can explain, with clear examples, how they have gone about practicing the art of success.

For example, if you are interviewing a person you think might be a high achiever, you can ask him or her this: "They say that all successful people make it a daily habit to practice some aspect of their success. Can you explain to me what you were practicing yesterday, as it relates to your goals, in as much detail as you can?" High achievers will be able to talk for an hour on that question. Low achievers, by contrast, won't have very much to say.

Practicing the Art of Happiness

Reviewing the thorough analyses of the traits of high-performing individuals in the works of Garfield and others, and comparing their discoveries to the findings of researchers such as Seligman, it seems reasonable to suggest that the daily practice of reaching for goals courageously, optimistically, and with faith is almost a sure-fire recipe for happiness, if a person is involved in a career that matters to him or her on a heart level. (In subsequent chapters we will give detailed information to show how people can align themselves with careers that are most suitable to their internal values or passions, as well as their individual personalities. As we will show, achieving a mind/heart balance in one's career is also critical if one is to sustain optimism for the long haul.)

Confucius beat many others to the punch on the point of optimism, or faith, as it applies to life and work, stating: "If people have no faith, I don't know what they [are] good for. Can a vehicle travel without a link to a source of power?"

Put another way, optimism, or faith—a deliberated, chosen belief that things will work out for the best if one wills them to—is like the gasoline in the engine of high-performing individuals. It is the fuel that makes everything else run.

Following is an example of the way a positive attitude affects the career of high performers. Some people tell me this is a story about optimism. Others tell me it is a story about persistence. I think it may be a story about both. I will let you decide.

The Woman Who Wouldn't Give Up

I think everyone has had a friend or acquaintance similar to the person I will write about here. I will call her Ariel. Now, I know that people such as my friend Ariel come in all shapes and sizes and ages, but they all have one thing in common: a depth of character and a will to succeed that makes it virtually impossible for them to ever give up once they set their minds on a goal.

When we were younger, Ariel reminded me a lot of that guy Rudy in the movie about the short, poor kid from the steel town who wanted to play football for Notre Dame. She had the same kind of personality. Only she had a different dream—

she wanted to dance at one of the nation's top schools for the performing arts. After pursuing her dreams as a dancer from early childhood, she tried out for the dance department at this prestigious school, and was turned down. But this was a decision that Ariel simply could not accept. After all, she'd been dreaming about going to this famous school every year since she was 5. After she was rejected, she went back to the head of the auditioning committee and requested another audition. They politely told her that she would only be disappointed, and they wanted to spare her any further pain. Ariel said they owed her another audition after all she had been through, and that if she didn't pass this one, she would walk away and never bother them again. The auditioning committee assured Ariel that her chances were beyond negligible—in fact, they said, she stood no chance of being admitted now. So, they said, they would have to regretfully decline her request for another audition. The next day Ariel came back and asked them if they could possibly change their mind about that decision, stating that she really, really, really would leave them alone if they gave her just one more chance.

"If you gave me one more opportunity to audition, and I fail, I promise I will go away and leave you alone," Ariel told them. "All I ask is that you give me just one more chance."

Realizing that Ariel would not go away until they met her request, the school agreed to give Ariel one more chance to be rejected. They agreed to let her come back in three weeks. At the end of that three weeks Ariel had lost another 10 pounds. She worked out in silence 15 hours a day preparing for her victory. On the day of the audition, she was all by herself on the same stage where she had been rejected last time. A small group of judges sat in three chairs watching her. When the last audition was over, and the final verdict was announced, she sobbed. Only a minority of people on earth would know what that kind of crying felt like. They had finally let her in, citing "heart." They said she had a lot of heart. She slept in late the next day, and then got up in the afternoon to start practicing again, and danced hard for the rest of her life. She is now a well-known choreographer.

Making a List of High-Achiever Traits

As I have studied people such as Ariel in my career, I have found that most of them possess certain strengths and levels of insight, in addition to the fundamental core traits we have outlined in our fundamentals list:

1. They have a deep understanding of their psychological strengths and weaknesses, and they make an attempt to improve their weaknesses. If asked to discuss their weaknesses, they can easily vocalize them. But they are just as knowledgeable about their strengths.

2. They know what they are afraid of, and are committed to overcoming their fears.

3. They rarely put money first in their lives, and are almost always driven by a superior passion that defines their personal focus, including their financial focus.

4. They are intelligent, but not overly confident in their intelligence. They tend to challenge their own best ideas.

5. They have certain core character traits that allow them to create a strong network of allies and supporters. These traits include reliability, follow-up, trustworthiness, and optimism or cheerfulness.

6. The success of high-performing individuals is in some ways a result of the energy and efforts of those people in their network whom they have inspired.

7. They have discovered that practicing reliability, trust-worthiness, and cheerfulness on a daily basis builds greater discipline and self-reliance. This habit of practicing character builds escalating patterns of success.

8. They lack a sense of entitlement and have a strong desire to prove their worth. This trait is apparent at all times and comes through in almost every communication they have with others, and in almost all of their actions.

9. They usually have a strong artistic or creative side, or have a genuine passion for solving problems. In many cases, they have both.

Questions That Get at Authenticity

Earlier in this book we discussed how the candidate can help you conduct a more effective interview by providing a written self-assessment. In order to keep the interview fluid and relaxed, however, you will want to have a few more simple questions you can ask as follow-ups to the more demanding process of investigating the candidate's accomplishments. Here are a few examples of the types of questions you might ask in order to get at the candidate's character strengths and authenticity.

Professional Pride

Question: When you look back at everything you have been able to accomplish in your entire life, what is the one event, the one moment in your career, in which you have felt the most pride in who you are as a person, as a leader, and as a good example to other people? Explain this in as much detail as you can.

Strength

Question: What is the most difficult challenge you have ever had to overcome, something that may have made other people give up? How hard did you have to try, and what kept you going? What were you fighting for?

Responsibility

Question: Have you ever experienced what it feels like to be someone's hero, or someone that another person looked up to? What kind of example of responsibility did you set in doing so?

Reputation

Question: What part of your character do you care about most deeply and passionately from a professional perspective? What part of your professional identity will you fight the hardest to uphold, defend, and preserve? Explain in detail how you have defended it in the past.

Passion

Question: Pick something you are extremely passionate about inside of work and tell me what interests you about it. Make me understand why you care about it. Tell me what it is that makes you remain committed to this cause or value.

Optimism

Question: What is the most interesting and uplifting thing you have learned this week about the potential goodness of people, as you have studied the way human beings act around you in the best of circumstances?

Empathy and Awareness

Question: Tell us about the best recent example of how you have had to become more flexible or tolerant with someone in the workplace in order to deal with a difficult person or situation. Tell us what you learned about the other person's challenges as you negotiated this difficult situation.

Purpose

Question: What has given you the greatest sense of pride and fulfillment in your career? Explain in detail, and tell us of the last time you experienced this level of pride and fulfillment.

Curiosity

Question: What is the best book that you have read lately in an area related to your career? Explain in detail what you liked about the book, and what you learned.

Strategic Thinking

Question: Explain in detail exactly what you would do the first two weeks on the job here, knowing what you currently know about the job as we have described it to you.

These are only a few examples of the kind of character-based questions you might ask to help uncover the core traits of your candidates, following the principles described in this book. For an extensive list of other excellent questions you might ask in a character-based interview, I highly recommend *Ask the Right Questions, Hire the Best People* by Ron Fry (Career Press, 2006).

To conclude this chapter neatly, let us restate one of its central themes: For high-performing individuals, optimism, or a positive outlook, is, to a large extent, a choice. Although some traits of positive thinking may exhibit themselves early, sustained optimism throughout a lifetime involves a practiced level of faith exercised on a daily basis—in choosing to believe that things will work out for the best as long as one maintains a positive outlook, and works persistently, even in the face of setbacks.

Ariel chose optimism when she could have chosen defeat. And her choice changed not only her life, but also the lives of hundreds of people she has mentored since that time, and thousands of human beings who have since been uplifted by her art.

In addition to optimism and persistence, job alignment drives and determines success. People do not tend to be optimistic if they are not in jobs that are somehow related to their passions and values. So, as we probe deeper into the hiring process, we are seeking to help the candidate make sure the job matches his or her motivations as closely as possible. Part of this process involves helping the candidate to carefully think about his or her professional values, and how those values are linked with his or her professional motivations. This is what we will discuss in the next chapter.

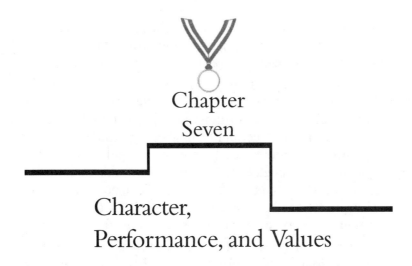

Chapter Seven

Character, Performance, and Values

One of the most thorough manuals on the competency-based hiring process is Bradford Smart's *Topgrading* (Penguin, 2005). Among many excellent points made in Smart's book is this: It is a deadly career mistake to accept a job or promotion that you are not really qualified for, or don't entirely want to do. Increased pay, recognition, or prestige won't matter if you talk yourself into taking a position in which you don't have the skills to succeed. I would add one thought to that by saying that it is just as dangerous to take a job when your heart isn't in it—when the job doesn't truly align with your authentic self and genuine motivations.

In this chapter we will present simple tools that can be used to engage candidates in a conversation about their real motivations in life, in order to see whether those motivations will be rewarded on the job, or thwarted. Persistence occurs, after all, when the rewards given for hard work are the rewards the employee is looking for on a deep, soulful level. The rewards most people are looking for are often more significant than money and prestige. They usually have something to do with passion. Passions rewarded make people persistent, plain and simple.

One of the real secrets to high performance, for any individual, is to make sure that he or she has fully investigated what truly motivates him or her from a heart perspective before deciding on a career. A certain truth about enlightened recruiting is this: We should all take the time to get to know our candidates well enough to make sure they are taking the job because that's where their heart is leading them, not just because they need a job and happen to have the skills. That is the quickest route to misery for them and under-productivity for you.

There are many excellent tools out there that I recommend candidates use in order to get a better feel for their true aspirations—what matters to their heart. That is what we will discuss in the next section.

Helping Candidates Assess Their Values

Employees tend to perform better when their jobs are aligned with their inner values. In the next section I will describe a few excellent tools that exist in the marketplace to help you and your candidates outline and assess the values that lead to the feeling of success when the job and employee are properly aligned with each other.

One values assessment tool I might recommend is a fairly simple but highly useful tool developed by an assessment company called Target Training International, based in Scottsdale, Arizona. The tool is called the Personal Attitudes, Interests, and Values instrument, and measures six values or passions known to be important to people in varying degrees. Though it is simple in concept, the factors measured represent what I continue to believe is a profoundly important rule in job satisfaction: people tend to feel most successful when their jobs are aligned with their inner values, not just their education or credentials.

The instrument has an interesting history in that it is based on the work of a German philosopher who, more than a century ago, provided a fascinating blueprint for studying the passions and values that underlie motivation and commitment to a career purpose.

An Unsung Values Hero

Not too many people have heard the name Eduard Spranger, except in Germany, where he is respected as a minor philosopher. In 1928, Spranger published a book that would largely fall into obscurity, titled *Types of Men*. In this brilliantly original work, Spranger broke with the psychological mold of people such as Freud and basically announced that he was more interested in what made people passionate than he was in neurosis or psychological disease. As such, Spranger actually had a lot in common with modern-day "positive" psychologists such as Martin Seligman and his peers, who are interested in the way coaching, counseling, and self-knowledge can help people create lives and careers that are connected with their authentic passions. As an early pioneer of such thinking, Spranger essentially proposed that people would feel most successful if the jobs they did during the day were somehow connected to their innate passions, or values. In other words, Spranger suggested that the "feeling of success" means different things for different people. Some people might feel successful if they are making a lot of money and have an "economic" passion. But if a person had more of a "social" passion and was essentially interested in making the world a better place, the mere acquisition of money would do absolutely nothing to give him or her a feeling of success in his or her heart, Spranger postulated.

When you look at the six measurable passions that Spranger identified, it becomes clear that he was talking about traits that were more related to the heart than to the head.

The passions he identified are:

1. The **Economic** Passion—People with this passion want to get the maximum reward for the amount of time and energy they invest in any project or endeavor. Most successful businesspeople have this as one of their dominant values.

2. The **Aesthetic** Passion—People who have the aesthetic (sometimes known as the artistic) passion as a predominant value have a love of beauty, form, and art. In some way they want to leave the world a more beautiful or artistically diverse place than they found it.

3. The **Theoretical** Passion—People who have the theoretical value or passion have a passion for the acquisition of knowledge. They often enjoy research, and like to write books and papers. They essentially like to know that they have explained things better than they have been explained before.

4. The **Social** Passion—People with the social value are passionate about helping others and would like to leave the world a better place than they found it.

5. The **Religious** Passion—People with the religious passion, as it was described by Spranger, are most passionate about the realm of their faith, and are mostly guided by what they feel are the dictates of God.

6. The **Political** Passion—People with the political passion are motivated most by the concept of acquiring power, social prestige, and control over others, whether in politics or another arena.

Spranger's work on values was eventually picked up by a person with a larger name in the history of psychology, Harvard's Gordon Allport, a founding father of personality psychology. Allport, a Harvard PhD, was a psychologist who viewed personality as composite of traits, characteristics, and attitudes. He held to the notion that the "self" was the foundation of personality, and that human beings are largely proactive in the sense that they are driven by their goals, purposes, plans, and moral values. Allport differed from Spranger in his outlook in that he believed the self was shaped by environmental forces—and he rejected Spranger's notion that the self was shaped by hereditary factors or genetics. In other words, Allport believed that a person's self was not predetermined, but could be changed if the person wanted to change. Nonetheless, Allport did borrow some of Spranger's ideas on values when he collaborated with P.E. Vernon and G. Lindzey to develop the journal *The Study of Values* in 1931, which was revised in 1951 and 1961, and which is still in use in some circles.

The Emergence of the Personal Attitudes, Interests, and Values Instrument

Using these same principles as yardsticks for measurement, Bill Bonnstetter and associates at Target Training International developed the Personal Attitudes, Interests, and Values instrument.

Based on his research and validation of the concepts in the workplace, Bonnstetter slightly altered two of the dimensions in Spranger's original model to better encompass passions and values that seemed to be connected with the feeling of success in modern-day jobs.

In Bonnstetter's model, the Economic Passion was renamed The "Utilitarian" Passion, which generally reflects the mental attitude of all "can-do" people who like to get things done and be rewarded for their efforts. The Religious Passion was renamed the "Traditional" value in Bonnstetter's construction, to describe people who have a passion for preserving tradition and culture in other areas besides religion, and the Political Passion was changed to "Independent," to reflect the degree to which a person likes to march to the beat of his or her own drum, so to speak.

Following is a simple explanation of the six values behind this values assessment model. It will be useful to examine this list to see which of the values would most likely motivate the ideal candidate for any job you are trying to fill. (Most people have at least two values high on their list.)

Six Core Measurable Values

1. I want to get the most reward possible on my investment of time, energy, and talent.

2. I want to help improve society and help the world to be a better place.

3. I want to help improve the beauty of the world or our appreciation of art and beauty.

4. I want to add to the knowledge of the world or increase the intellectual capital of the world.

5. I want to help preserve the tradition and culture of the institutions or places I hold dear.

6. I want to carve out an independent life for myself and march to the beat of my own drum.

(Value 6, called the independent value, usually manifests itself through one of the other values. For example, people with high independence usually express it through one of the other values; in other words, they are fiercely independent in their research, or have a fierce desire to be independent as an artist, and so forth.)

The Six Business Motivators: A Deeper Explanation of Values in the Workplace

One of the nation's foremost consultants on the subjects of behavioral assessment and values assessment in the workplace is Bill Schult, Senior, the president of Maximum Potential, an assessment and consulting firm based in St. Paul, Minnesota.

Based on decades of research and practice, Schult has created a model for analyzing values as "business motivators." The values assessment framework and tools he has developed are extremely useful for helping individuals look at the underlying motivations that drive their professional momentum. The same model is equally useful for helping businesses analyze the motivations that drive their teams.

In the following section, Schult describes his research and his model in his own words. It's an excellent synopsis of the way values influence behavior in the workplace. It will also give you a much deeper understanding of the relevance of the six values described previously.

♛ ♛ ♛

The Six Business Motivators

By Bill Schult, Sr., president, Maximum Potential

Motivators, simply put, are a collection of learned attitudes and beliefs. Psychologists often refer to the motivators as the initiators of behavior. There are many attitudes and beliefs that help each of us define how we view the world. It is these attitudes and beliefs that ultimately become our internal motivators. It has been said that all true motivation comes from within. Motivators add depth and dimension to behavior by providing insight into why we do what we do. They are what get us out of bed in the morning. They are why we work! It is our internal motivators that provide each of us with the most rewarding satisfaction in our work and personal lives. Individuals and corporations use motivators for goal-setting, management, team-building, decision-making, and other important areas throughout an organization.

We respond to other types of motivation in our work and lives as well. The first is "superimposed" motivation. This type of motivation is external in form. It is motivation that is learned, but it is not as personally rewarding or as long lasting as internal motivation. An example of a superimposed motivator is the person who has friends and business associates with lots of money (High Economic Motivator), and he/she feels the need to do well financially to keep up, when in reality, he/she would prefer to live in a smaller home (High Social Motivator) with less amenities, and help out at the local food shelves. This type of motivator does not result in the satisfaction of a person's internal motivators, and is generally short lived.

Another type of motivation is known as "repressed" internal motivation. These are usually motivators that we want to act on, but for one reason or another we cannot. We have made a conscious decision to act on other motivators at the present time. An example of a repressed internal motivator is the person who wants to write or paint (High Aesthetic Motivator), but who realizes it may be years before he/she makes any money to provide for him-/herself, so he/she takes a job (Economic) he/she may not like in order to provide a living.

Many people never satisfy their repressed internal motivators; still others find alternate avenues to satisfy them. People who are the most productive, satisfied, and pleased with their lives are those who truly satisfy their internal motivators.

Motivators can be flexible, and will often change throughout our careers and lives. As an individual's situation changes, the priorities of his/her motivators tend to change also. What tends to happen with motivators is that as one motivator is satisfied, another moves to the fore. This is often referred to as "motivational shift." Individuals may experience as many as five or six motivational shifts throughout their lifetimes. Studies have shown that the intensity of each of these motivators, in terms of importance, is determined by our personal priorities at a given time in our careers and lives.

Business Motivators measure six motivators based on psychologist Eduard Spranger's book *Types of Men*. These motivators are defined as Conceptual, Aesthetic, Economic, Power and Authority, Social, and Doctrine.

Motivators, similar to behavior, can be viewed in degrees of intensity. Each of the six motivators in the Business Motivators model is charted on a 100-point scale. Each of the six Business Motivators is normed, and an individual's Business Motivators results are charted against the respective norms.

The farther an individual's score is from a specific motivator's norm, the greater emotional investment an individual has in that particular motivator. Having a motivator with a score below the 50th percentile on the graphic scale does not necessarily indicate that an individual has little interest or emotional feeling invested in this motivator, but that at the present time it has a lesser priority. Individuals will often have more difficulty understanding the motivators of others that are very different from their own.

Motivators tend to travel in pairs. The two motivators that are most important to an individual at a given time appear to complement each other to create a certain effect. Motivators that are in an individual's bottom group, and probably have been since they were young, generally have little or no motivational influence on an individual.

Let's look at the six Business Motivators to develop a better understanding of each of them. What does a high score in each motivator mean, and what does a low score in each motivator mean?

Conceptual

Individuals who place a greater priority on this motivator can be identified as those who are in search of fact and reality. They are objective and critical, while seeking to separate fact from opinion. They are interested in the logical progression of reasoning. These individuals attempt to order and classify knowledge through investigation and validation. They often prefer ideas, concepts, or things, to people.

Individuals who place a lesser priority on this motivator tend to form opinions rather than using facts. They prefer to trust their instincts and do not feel the need for excessive study or investigation. They will often accept the conclusions of others at face value. They feel more comfortable dealing with the emotions of people rather than the science of factual investigation.

Economic

Individuals who place a greater priority on this motivator share a common interest in economic gain. They are interested in what is useful in the business world of production, marketing, consumption of goods, and generation of profit. In a business setting they strive for positive results and profit. They are motivated to achieve monetary gain.

Individuals who place a lesser priority on this motivator are not driven to accumulate wealth and material things. They do not use such things as a measure of their success. They will work to achieve a standard of living that is acceptable to them. In business, their main concern is service and support.

Aesthetic

Individuals who place a greater priority on the Aesthetic motivator have a visual awareness of their environment. They have a strong sense of color, form, beauty, and symmetry. A higher priority, however, does not suggest that the individual has creative or artistic talents. They experience pleasure in an environment that is aesthetically appealing in nature and man-made creations, simply for the mental and emotional stimulation they provide.

People who place a lesser priority on this motivator tend to be more practical. They are not necessarily interested in things having form, function, and artistic beauty. They can live in their environment as it is and have little interest in changing it. They judge things by their utility.

Power and Authority

Individuals who place a greater priority on this motivator enjoy being influential and in positions of power. These individuals are willing to take the risks involved in accepting a leadership role. They want the authority to be in command, and to exercise management functions and responsibilities. They display the material trappings that demonstrate success and accomplishment. These individuals are energized by competition, to be first or most respected in a given arena, including business.

Individuals who place a lesser priority on this motivator feel that having power and authority is not worth the adversities one must face to gain them. They are aware of the risks involved in leadership roles. It is important to note that these individuals will be supportive of causes behind the scenes and will enjoy contributing to an organization's success. They do not seek public recognition of their work and accomplishments.

Social

Individuals who place a greater priority on the Social motivator exhibit a genuine concern for others. They feel that giving equal opportunity to people enhances an organization. These individuals seek to improve the welfare of others. They have a strong sense of social justice, and prefer to set themselves apart from others based on their efforts to help those seen as less fortunate.

Individuals who place a lesser priority on this motivator tend to be more restrained in their concern for the welfare of others. They feel an organization should not have an obligation to provide others with an advantage. They believe everyone should get what he or she deserves. These individuals generally think that extra effort and hard work lead to success. They will help others, but only when they feel others can no longer help themselves.

Doctrine

Individuals who place a greater priority on this motivator have a strong belief system centered on tradition and customs. They see things from a moral and philosophical point of view. They seek to conduct their lives and business activities within a system of accepted principles and standards. They are generally seen as traditionalists.

Individuals who place a lesser priority on this motivator tend to be independent thinkers and non-traditionalists. They feel comfortable making decisions apart from established codes, traditions, or customs. They prefer to be seen as nonconformists, who do not seek to impose their moral standards and principles on others.

♟

Helping Candidates Talk About Their Values

It is extremely helpful in the interview process for you and the candidate to spend some time talking about his or her passions and values. As an exercise, ask the candidate to review the following list and pick the two choices he or she identifies with most, in order of priority. Write his or her answers down for use as discussion points later.

1. I want to get the most reward possible on my investment of time, energy, and talent. (Utilitarian or Economic)

2. I want to help improve society and help the world to be a better place. (Social)

3. I want to help improve the beauty of the world or our appreciation of art and beauty. (Aesthetic)

4. I want to add to the knowledge of the world or increase the intellectual capital of the world. (Theoretical)

5. I want to help preserve the tradition and culture of the institutions or places I hold dear. (Traditional)

6. I want to carve out an independent life for myself and march to the beat of my own drum. (Independent)

The Candidate's Primary Passions:

_____

Now, considering the passions the candidate has identified, ask how he or she envisions that the job you are interviewing for will enable him or her to use those passions (and the talents connected with them). Again, passions drive motivation. Is the candidate sure he or she will be motivated by the job, or is he or she just saying so?

This may be one of the most important questions to get to the bottom of, and can't be ignored. As Spranger and others have suggested, the fulfillment of passions, along with the fulfillment of "ego needs," may be the greatest predictor of long-term happiness in any job. With that in mind, we will continue this analysis in the next chapter by discussing how the ego needs of the candidate might affect the hiring process, and how both you and the candidate can be even more careful before saying yes to the job.

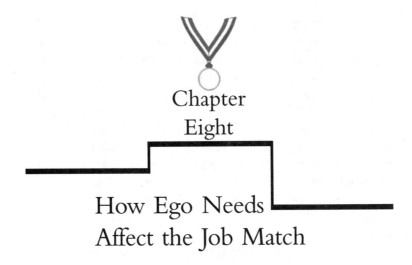

Chapter
Eight

How Ego Needs
Affect the Job Match

Now that we have investigated the measurable passions that are connected with personal investment on the job, let's consider another key set of factors—the psychological motivators.

Workplace psychology is largely about fear and reward. If we are in the wrong role, wrong culture, or wrong environment, or if our psychological needs are not met, our fears are magnified, we are unhappy, and we tend to under-perform.

Therefore, it is important to know what makes people tick from a psychological standpoint. The following explanation of behavioral psychology as it applies to the workplace will serve a triple role: It will help you carry on deeper conversations with candidates about their psychological drivers, it will help you ask better questions about their fit for the job, and it will help you be a better communicator with existing employees who have a completely different personality than you—a key component of emotional intelligence in leadership.

Most employers are familiar with a tool called the DISC inventory, a four-factor assessment that looks at drive, influencing ability (friendliness), steadfastness, and conscientiousness (compliance). Although the DISC was never created as selection tool, per se, and should not be used as one, it can be invaluable as a discussion tool for the following reason: The DISC assessment (and there are numerous vendors of it in the marketplace) renders a graph that shows what a person's *natural style* is (whether they were born driven and friendly, for example), and what their *adapted style* in the workplace is. If any of the measures on a person's adapted style comes across as significantly lower or higher than in his or her natural style, he or she may well have been under much stress in his or her last job, or under a lot of stress in the current one, if he or she happens to be your employee. Marked changes in the adapted style may mean that candidates are twisting themselves out of shape to conform to a job that is really not suited for them. Or it may mean other things: If people's drive seems to be dropping in the workplace, they may be having issues with motivation or sense of purpose. Can you ask them what that might be? If their friendliness score is dropping, they may be having issues with morale. That could be a point of discussion too. So, in most instances, if your goal is to build and sustain high-performing work teams, I highly recommend using the DISC inventory as a discussion tool for candidates (to discuss alignment concerns) and existing team members (to discuss stress, morale, or motivational concerns).

Following is a brief tour through the dimensions of this four-factor behavioral model, along with suggestions for how you can use this assessment and the principles behind it for better candidate interviews, internal communications, and team-building.

Basic Behavioral Psychology in the Workplace

Research shows that when we are examining the behavioral or visible characteristics that any one of us brings to a career or life in general, it is possible to separate the aspects of our behavior into four general categories. These categories are not sacrosanct or all-inclusive, but they do provide a useful guide when we are trying to understand our own behavior and the behavior of others. The four-factor behavioral model shows that all of us possess the four following behavioral traits to varying degrees.

1. **Drive or Ambition.** All of us have some ambition or drive. Drive, or ambition, is a biologically rooted trait, and stems from our need to seek out new experiences. Research has shown that some of us have more of this trait than others. For some of us, the quality of ambition or drive, the need to seek out new experiences and to achieve new goals (sometimes referred to as the desire to conquer), will be our predominant trait. In other words, some of us will have more of this quality than we do the other behavioral qualities. If we do have more of this trait, it will largely influence the way other people view us, and it will also influence the way we view ourselves and other people. For example, if you have more ambition or drive than your neighbor, you will probably feel that other people are somewhat lacking in ambition or drive and are less energetic than you are. On the other hand, people in your life who have less of the quality of ambition or drive may well view you as someone who is somewhat arrogant, self-centered, and a little too ambitious. Obviously, none of these perceptions can be regarded as the "truth" about you or anyone else. These are merely perceptions that are created in the minds of all human beings as they attempt to understand the motives behind the behaviors of people who are different than they are.

    The same rule applies to the other three predominant behavioral traits listed here.

2. **Influencing Ability or Friendliness.** Influencing ability, or friendliness, stems from a basic human need to be appreciated, accepted, and approved by others. All of us have this trait to some degree. However, some of us have it to a larger degree than others. People for whom this is a predominant trait generally have a greater need than others to be accepted and approved, and therefore, this predominant trait will greatly shape and influence the way they view other people and the way other people view them. That is, if you have this trait to a large degree, you consistently have the impression that other people do not appreciate you as much as they should. And your friends who have this trait to a lesser degree may simply feel that you need to be appreciated too much, or have an exaggerated need for approval and acceptance. In other words, people who have this quality as their predominant trait will often be viewed as "needy."

3. **Emotional Stability or Steadfastness.** People who possess this as their predominant trait have an inborn need for security and safety. They do not like to make quick or rash decisions, and they like to live lives, more or less, that are defined by stability and prudence. People who have this trait to a predominant degree may feel that other people who are not similar to them are lacking in prudence, and are not living the kind of lives that generate security and stability. Conversely, the friends and coworkers of such people may have the impression that highly steadfast people are a little bit too safe and need to loosen up a little bit and take more risks.

4. **Conscientiousness or Compliance.** Conscientiousness or compliance seems to stem from an inborn need to be accurate, right, and careful. People who possess these traits to a predominant degree seem to be more meticulous and painstaking than others, and have a high regard for facts, accuracy, and a methodical approach to both

life and business. People who have this trait to a predominant degree may feel that others who are not like them are somewhat sloppy in their thinking and inattentive to details. Conversely, the friends and coworkers of such people often tend to feel that highly conscientious people can be both nit-picky and self-righteous at the same time.

Admittedly, we all have a complex mixture of these traits, but some of us have one of the traits to a greater degree than we do the others, and this is called our predominant trait. Our predominant trait largely determines how we will act under stress. If the ego needs of the predominant style are not being met, the person feels anxious and stressed out. This is the heart of emotional intelligence—understanding what people need in terms of their ego, and the way they like to be interacted with and listened to. Here are a few general rules:

+ People with a high level of drive or ambition fear being viewed as unimportant, or being in unimportant jobs.

+ People who are highly influencing or friendly fear being left out of the crowd, or not being appreciated.

+ People who are highly steadfast fear losing their job security or financial security, and they also do not tolerate constant change very well.

+ People who are highly conscientious fear being wrong.

So, understanding the ego needs, communication styles, and fears of the four basic predominant behavioral styles can be enormously useful in helping all of us to improve our communications with candidates and employees. Here are a few simple guidelines that may be useful.

Emotional Intelligence 101

1. When working with driven/ambitious people (extravert type 1), don't say anything to make them feel unimportant. Do everything you can do to make them feel *more* important.

2. When working with friendly/influencing people (extravert type 2, sometimes known as a "relater"), do not do anything to make them feel excluded or left out. Do everything possible to make them feel more included.

3. When working with steadfast people (introvert type 1), don't do or say anything to make them feel less safe or less financially secure, or that you are jeopardizing the security and safety of their loved ones. Do anything possible help them see that you are interested in and care about their security.

4. When working with the highly conscientious or compliant type (introvert type 2), don't do or say anything to make them feel that you do not care about accuracy and facts. Do everything possible to make them feel that you do care very much about being careful, accurate, and factual.

Most high-performing individuals in the business world are savvy communicators and have these rules of emotional intelligence down pat.

From a selection perspective, it can also be very useful to show candidates the following list of behavioral types and ask them what sounds most similar to them, simply to try to help them get a better idea of what makes them tick, and what stresses them out.

One way to get a deeper understanding of candidates' potential cultural fit is to ask them how they get along with the different types in the workplace. For example, you could ask,

"How do you get along with highly ambitious, driven, CEO-types? Do you feel comfortable working with them? What is a type of person you enjoy working with most? What type of person do you least enjoy working with?" These questions will not only help you to gain insight into the type of environment your candidates will prefer, but will also help you to gain greater insight into the type customers they may be most comfortable dealing with as well.

To find out what a candidate's predominant style might be, you could review the following list and ask the candidate which type of the four sounds the most similar to him or her, and why. Alternatively, you could ask him or her which are the top two descriptions that resemble him or her most, and why.

1. I am **Driven**. More than anything else I want to know that what I do is important, and that other people know it is important too.

2. I am **Influencing/Friendly** (a relater). More than anything else I want to be part of the in-crowd, part of the team, and accepted by a circle of supportive friends and colleagues.

3. I am a **Steadfast** person. More than anything I want to protect the financial security of myself, my family, and my loved ones.

4. I am a **Conscientious** person. More than anything else, I want to be accurate, careful, and right.

Are They Being Authentic or Just Telling You What You Want to Hear?

After your candidates choose the statement (or top two statements) that they most identify with, ask them to explain what stressed them out in their last jobs as a result of these traits, and how they dealt with it, giving specifics. If, for example, your candidates are highly conscientious types, they will be able to tell you the frustrations they may have experienced in helping to improve accuracy and attention to detail in their last jobs. By asking questions about stress in the context of behavioral style, you can get a much clearer picture of what the candidates' ego needs are, and how they have dealt with stress in previous jobs in which their strengths and weaknesses were tested. Highly driven people have great strengths as pioneers and innovators, but they tend to become miserable if they don't feel important, or in charge. Highly social people have great strengths as motivators and team leaders, but if placed in isolated jobs with a low chance for interaction, they tend to wilt. Highly steadfast people are dependable as employees, but any sign of risk, change, or instability tends to make them uncomfortable. Highly conscientious people are fastidious, and great at helping maintain quality and accuracy, but when they are put in environments where the rules are fast and loose, they quit.

Again, all of us possess the traits of ambition, friendliness, steadfastness, and conscientiousness to some degree, but it is important for candidates to discuss how much these traits influence their behavior and happiness in the workplace. Asking candidates to explain what causes them the most stress not only helps us to understand how they handle stress, it also helps us to better understand what type of job or environment might be best for them.

Bear in mind that when you ask many people what stresses them out the most, you will typically get answers such as "uncertainty." That is a valid response—stress certainly does stem from uncertainty. But the deeper question is: Uncertainty about what? About losing your financial security? About not having a stable job? About not being appreciated? About not being in an important role? About not knowing whether your company is going to pass the next audit? Knowing what stresses the candidate or employee, and what type of uncertainties causes them the greatest distress, will give you a much deeper knowledge of their job fit.

But as we will discuss in the next section, a more complete portrait of candidate motivation can be obtained by looking at how the candidate's ego needs and values interact to influence the choice of an optimum career path.

How Values and Psychology Both Play a Role in Job Happiness

Earlier we talked about values and alignment, and in the previous section we talked about behavior and alignment. My next goal is to show that both values and psychology intermingle in the candidate to create highly unique motivations—and thus highly unique ideal job fits. The following example will explain how this is so.

I have a good friend and colleague, whom I will call Rachael, who is a prominent psychologist. She has two very smart and attractive children, whom I will call Naomi and Aaron.

From a behavioral standpoint, Aaron and Naomi are similar. They are both type 2 extraverts, and by this I mean they are *relaters*. They are what some behaviorists would call influencing/friendly people. Both Aaron and Naomi like people, and want to feel that they belong to a group. They like fitting in, and they seek approval. They like to know that they are part of the happening scene. And if they ever felt they were being left out of the crowd, they would become sad. They like relating to people, they enjoy crowds, and they like conversation. From a psychological standpoint, the worst thing you could do to Aaron or Naomi would be to make them feel that they were not part the group. So, from a behavioral standpoint, they are very much alike. They both need to be in careers in which they feel they are members of a team, are accepted in a group, and get the chance to interact with lots of people. That is what makes them similar. But, in helping Aaron and Naomi make the best career decision, it is just as important to talk about what makes them different. And in terms of their passions—or their heart-centered values—Aaron and Naomi are as different as night and day.

Naomi's Heart vs. Aaron's Heart

Although both Naomi and Aaron are card-carrying *relaters*, they differ greatly in terms of their values. Naomi, in terms of her values, or passions, is highly socially conscious, whereas Aaron is highly utilitarian or economic. The difference is profound.

Naomi, because of her love of and desire to help people, and her **social improvement** value set, may be best suited to be a doctor, nurse, psychologist, counselor, social activist, or any other type job that helps her feel that she is alleviating human suffering in some way. If she did not have the chance to nurture this social passion in her job, she would become miserable, no matter how much money she was making, or whatever trappings of success she might earn.

Aaron, because of his love of and desire to help people, and his extremely high **economic** or **utilitarian** value set, and his love of business, is born to be a CEO, financial advisor, or some type of business leader who has the opportunity to acquire wealth while helping other people become more successful. Deprived of such an opportunity to nurture this duality created by the balance of his personality and his passion, Aaron would wilt as well.

Now that we have fully analyzed the process for helping create an alignment between the values of the candidate and the motivators of the job, let's consider the key questions that employers would want to ask themselves as a result of studying the information in this chapter.

Management Checklist for Motivating Different Types of Employees:
Key Questions for Peak-Performing Companies

- ✖ What does your company do to reward people who want the maximum return (often financial) on the amount of energy they invest in their jobs during the day?

- ✖ What does your company do to reward those people who want to improve society in some way?

- ✖ What does your company do to reward those people who want to make an aesthetic or artistic contribution?

- ✖ What does your company do to reward those people who want to add to the intellectual capital of the world?

- ✖ What does your company do to reward those people who want to help preserve important aspects of tradition and culture—which may include the tradition and culture of the company?

- ✖ What does your company do to reward those people who want to achieve a measure of independence?

- ✖ What does your company do to reward those people who need to know that what they do is important?

- ✖ What does your company do to reward those people who need to feel included?

- ✖ What does your company do to reward those people who need to know that their security matters to the company?

- ✖ What does your company do to reward those people who tirelessly work to maintain high standards of accuracy?

If you have developed a specific process to help and answer all of these simple questions, you are probably close to achieving your initial goals in balancing employee fulfillment with organizational performance.

If you do not have succinct answers to these questions, it may be time to form the teams and focus groups that will be necessary to address these questions, provide simple answers that employees can understand, set clear expectations based on these answers, and create whatever additional incentives seem appropriate if the answers do not yet exist.

In closing, before we move on, let us reiterate our main point in this chapter: The issue of *career identity* is a critical step of definition for most people. Everyone wants to know *who they are* and *why they matter*. It is usually the most important thing to most people.

So, if you can help people do that, by using any of the simple tools in this chapter, or any similar ones that work well for you, then you will have gone a long way toward helping your people bring greater meaning and energy into their jobs. And that will invariably translate into greater performance for the team. It will also help you to become highly regarded as a manager among those you are seeking to coach—and to make a profound difference in the world yourself.

With that in mind, let us proceed to Part II, where we take all that we learned in the first part to a higher level by focusing on a few simple actions that brilliant managers can take to create cultures of greatness.

PART II

Creating

Cultures of

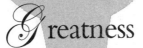

Greatness

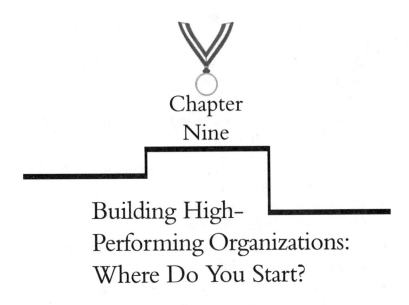

Chapter Nine

Building High-Performing Organizations: Where Do You Start?

B eing a good manager is a tough job. If you are a good manager, you already know that. There are hard choices and accountability measures that come with being a good manager, which most people would not relish. In other words, being a good manager is not for the faint of heart. However, it is important to stress that most good managers see the importance of trying to work with or challenge people whose performance is not all that is desired, instead of firing people before the real reasons for their underperformance have been carefully studied and addressed. People underperform for many different reasons. In some cases, people may underperform on purpose, because of management issues and morale. Many factors must be taken into account before a decision is made that a person just won't cut it.

Good managers help their people discover and fix the things that are holding them back. But in order for them to be able to help their people improve, the team members must first trust that the manager is credible. To be a more effective manager, and keep more of your employees sticking around, you need to help create the greatest possible perception of your trustworthiness.

Most employees are looking to know that their managers possess the following traits:

- ✕ They have earned their stripes as producers in the area they are currently managing.

- ✕ They tend to give people the benefit of the doubt, until their team members make it impossible.

- ✕ They are easy to approach and will do anything to help their team members meet objectives.

- ✕ They provide the necessary training and resources for team members to meet those objectives.

- ✕ They are tough but fair—and always polite and encouraging.

- ✕ They possess great insight about people, and have a genuine desire to see other people succeed. In other words, they have a greater concern for the success of the team than they do for their own glory or upward-mobility—and everyone knows it.

If you are a great manager, you already know that great managers drive everything: They drive commitment, they drive loyalty, they drive performance, and they drive retention. If you are a great manager, you also know that coaching is everything. So, in this chapter, we will spend some time discussing how your own management and coaching efforts can help improve the retention rates and performance of the people you have struggled so hard to hire.

One of the philosophies that is most important to keep in mind during the process of improving any workforce is this: it is necessary to *pick the best*, and then *challenge the rest*. What I mean is that no matter how much effort you expend in selecting the very best people as new hires, you still have to contend with existing members of the workforce who may not have been hired with the same expectations of skill and potential as your new hires. This especially applies to companies that have set higher expectations and accountabilities for teams, and who have decided to improve their selection process as part of that goal.

The first phase of good coaching is to establish credibility by continuously setting the example of excellence in front of your people. Your high performers, in particular, will be watching your every move. They will be looking to you for continuous guidance because they want to continuously learn, grow, and improve. You and your managerial colleagues are the front line— you are the ones who are ultimately setting the standard of character for the entire company. If your people always see you modeling the character traits you would prefer them to display— for example, confidence, reliability, and self-reliance—then they will be far more likely to display those characteristics themselves.

Remember the anecdotes that I shared about the Marines earlier. In that part of the book I mentioned that when I showed a Marine recruiter a list of some of the most important character traits we are looking for in certain jobs, he mentioned that the Marine Corps looks for a very similar list of traits in the people it seeks to recruit. The Marine Corps also has an extensive program to help recruits work on and develop the particular strengths or traits on which they think they need to work. But, as we discussed then, the key to the effectiveness of "success modeling" in the Marines is this:

Marines would not respect their drill sergeant in boot camp—or learn anything at all from their drill sergeant—if they didn't know that the drill sergeant had "earned his stripes" and had gone through the same experiences the recruits were being asked to go through. In other words, the recruit has to know that the drill sergeant already possesses the qualities of grit and character the recruits are being asked to display, and is a living model and embodiment of those traits.

In corporate leadership and management, the same kind of modeling must take place if you are to first select and then retain high performers. High performers will only stay if they respect the people who are managing them, and they will only respect the people who are managing them if they feel that the manager is a living example of the traits they are being asked to emulate. So, again, the great manager must always possess:

- ✦ All of the traits you want your high-performing team members to possess.

- ✦ Additional leadership traits that will enable them to model, coach, train, and measure the performance of those traits in the people they supervise.

Helping Your Team Aspire to Excellence

In the first part of this book we focused on how you can improve your overall selection process—a topic we will continue to discuss. One question that always arises when people set out to improve their selection process is this: What do I do about the lower-performing individuals we happened to hire before this improved selection process was implemented? Obviously, you would not and should not set out to dismiss everyone who was hired before you improved your selection process or set higher expectations for both new hires and existing hires. Certainly, there will be many team members on your existing staff whom you will want to keep, even if they do need tons of help. For those with less than excellent performance, you may simply ask them to try and rise to the occasion and give a visible and renewed effort to modeling higher levels of achievement. As you do this, you may want bear in mind the experiences they could have had with a previous manager. If their previous manager was a bad manager—incommunicative, unsupportive, and weak in providing feedback or direction—there could be any number of reasons the employee seems lost or lethargic.

If that is what happened to them, and you are their new manager, you may be able to fix a lot of things quickly. In any working environment, team members tend to thrive when they are continuously educated and mentored, especially when managers can help them identify the personality traits or working habits that might be holding them back. If you are that kind of manager, you will not only help *select* champions, you will help build them.

In helping to build them, of course, you will need to help them build meaningful action plans for professional growth. Helping your team members build meaningful action plans for growth starts with setting expectations and clearly explaining how the areas you are asking them to improve will help the company improve as well. Helping employees to better understand, in fact, how their own action plans for improvement will affect the company's goals is one of the best things you can do to improve trust and collaboration.

With this in mind, let's consider a few methodical approaches you can take to help your team members see where it is they need to go.

Thought Exercise for Managers: Mapping Expectations

In order to get at the issues that will most readily yield meaningful individual action plans for your team members, it is always necessary to first map out the goals of the company and compare them with the goals of your department.

The following exercise may sound simple, but I have found it useful in helping managers to find a solid starting place for improving the effectiveness, morale, and skill sets of their team members.

First write down the three areas of improvement that you would like to see most in your own organization:

Area 1: _____

    Now answer this question:

    Why do we need this improvement?

_____

Area 2: _____

    Why do we need this improvement?

_____

Area 3: _____

    Why do we need this improvement?

_____

———

The answers you have provided to those questions help you continuously keep in mind the high-level overview of where you feel you need to go as an organization. It is the answers to these questions that help you to develop organizational action plans. But perhaps most importantly, it is the answers to these questions that help you keep your center as a leader. These are the questions that help you always keep your eyes on the prize.

But, as you know, organizational action plans only work when they are seamlessly integrated with the action plans of the various departments supporting the organization. Therefore, the second set of questions that guide the process of building high-performing organizations would be as follows:

———

1.   What is the first key area of improvement we would like to see among the members of our department as a whole?

_____

Why do we need this improvement?

_____

2. What is the second most important area of improvement we would like to see among the members of our department as a whole?

_____

Why do we need this improvement?

_____

3. What is the third most important area of improvement we would like to see among the members of our department as a whole?

_____

Why do we need this improvement?

_____

The answers to these questions are the answers that help us make the necessary plans to sharpen our competitive edge in terms of the force, or energy, that drives results. Organizational action plans provide the direction for improving the competitive edge. Departmental action plans create the steps that will be necessary to implement the changes.

However, it will not be possible to actually implement those steps without meticulously zeroing in on the areas of training and development that each member of the team needs in order to play the most effective role in the efforts of the team as a whole. And it will not be possible for team members to work on the areas they need the most help in unless:

✦ Someone has helped them to assess what those areas of needed improvement are.

✦ They are working with a manager who is capable of motivating, mentoring, and teaching them.

Thus, the four most important questions to ask at the initial stage of building high-performance teams are:

1. What tools and assessments (employee surveys, competency-based assessments, interviews, performance evaluations, and so on) have you used so far to ascertain what the most needed areas of development are for each individual team member in your department?

2. What are the first areas of most-needed improvement you would like to see for each individual?

3. How do you plan, from an individual or group training effort, to address those needs? And how do you plan to communicate your expectations to each individual? Do you already have the kind of relationship that will enable them to listen and care?

4. Are you working with other managers who are capable of teaching and educating their team members on these areas so that continuous forward momentum takes place? If your people are coming into contact with other managers that may be destroying your leadership efforts somehow, have you taken any steps to address that issue?

Question number four, from the perspective of organizations I have worked with, is critical. In fact, in many organizations I have studied where retention issues were a serious problem, it was clearly identified that a significant number of managers were lacking in people skills and mentoring skills. (There were some good managers in place, but the bad managers were ruling the day.) This is why the assessment of managerial teams from the standpoint of competency in coaching and mentoring skills is paramount to organizational success. You may be a good manager, but how many of your colleagues are? And does the executive branch even know who is who? Is anyone doing anything about it?

Ultimately, the key to retention is this: When employees feel they are receiving respectful and helpful interaction with their managers, they tend to stay. When they feel that they are not receiving respectful and helpful interaction with their managers, they tend to leave. So, if you are concerned about the overall welfare of your company, you have to be concerned about the overall composition of your entire management team.

From a practical standpoint, then, the three most critical questions to ask about your management team are:

1. How many of your managers would you say have excellent communication and coaching skills?

2. For those managers who do not have excellent coaching and communications skills, what programs have been implemented to help them improve those skills?

3. What tools, assessments, or processes have been implemented to help your company predict that you are hiring managers who already have excellent communication and coaching skills?

Some organizations simply do not know, keep track of, or do anything about the answers to the preceding questions. And because of that, attrition issues will continue to be a problem for them. Those that do focus on hiring and developing managers with excellent communication and coaching skills, however, are always more successful—their productivity is better and their people stay longer.

Coaching With Assessment and Metrics

The best way to develop coaching and training efforts for team members is to be as thorough as possible in your evaluations of your team members, and to use several different tracks for assessing developmental needs, including the use of competency-based assessments, but also incorporating internal performance data.

Try to imagine that you could fix every problem in your team overnight. What would you do from a training and development perspective if you could do everything? Now that you know what everything is, consider this: what would you do first, say, tomorrow by 7 a.m.?

We will assume a best-case scenario for training and development for your team around those goals as we ponder the following questions. In doing so, we will also assume that you already have chosen and implemented some type of assessment or survey (perhaps validated tests or surveys) to discover where your people rank in terms of skill level for others in the profession, and where they might need the most help developmentally.

Interrelated tracks of analysis that will help you put together the best possible training and development programs for your team members are as follows:

---

1. What is the single most important metric of performance (for example, raw data on sales goals met, and customer service satisfaction scores) that most powerfully ties in with your business goals?

---

2. What is the single most important skill you would most like to see your team members improve in order to achieve better results on those metrics?

---

3. Is there any kind of challenging assignment you might give to them as homework, to gauge their desire to learn and improve on this one skill? If so, what would that assignment be?

---

4. How would you measure the quality of their efforts in addressing this assignment?

    _____

5. What are the most effective training programs you have implemented lately as a manager?

    _____

6. What are the most effective strategies you have employed in one-on-one coaching? What results have you obtained from your coaching efforts so far?

    _____

7. What can you do to build on the training and coaching efforts you have put forth?

    _____

8. Equally importantly, what goals have you set for yourself to improve your own effectiveness as a coach and mentor? Do you want to be a better communicator? Do you want to spend more time with your people? Do you want to portray more energy and enthusiasm on the job yourself? What is your own action plan?

    _____

Here's an example of how we put this practice of multi-track assessment into action with a sales force.

The overall goal of our development and training effort was to increase the abilities of all salespeople to better communicate the competitive advantages of the company's services to the client. During the process of discovery we found that there was indeed a correlation between scores on tests of sales competency and scores on homework assignments that were given to test an understanding of corporate sales messages. By studying the response time on the completion of the exercises (how long it took them to complete), and what the quality of the response was, we were able to draw definite conclusions on two things:

1. How much additional training each member needed in order to get a better understanding of the company's sales messages.

2. What developmental aspects each individual needed most help with, and in what order—overcoming procrastination, becoming more self-reliant, creating a better time-management system, and so on.

The Marine Model of Coaching

The way the Marines go about preparing their recruits for the coaching experience is illuminating and psychologically instructive, especially from a candidate-attraction standpoint. Some of the character traits that are important to the Marines (which also reflect the character traits of top performers) are self-reliance and self-discipline.

When a candidate is interviewing with the Marine Corps, he or she is asked to self-rate him- or herself on the character traits that the Marine Corps is looking for.

For example, the Corps will ask something similar to this:

Marine Question 1: "How would you currently rate yourself in the area of self-discipline?"

Once the candidate answers this question (and recruits are asked to answer as truthfully as possible), he or she is asked a series of other fascinating questions:

Marine Question 2: "How do you think that a level of less than optimal self-discipline may have held you back, or put obstacles in the path of your success so far?"

Marine Question 3: "If you were to maintain that same level of self-discipline and never improve, how far behind do you think you will fall, in terms of the goals you would like to achieve throughout the next five years?"

Once the Marine recruit answers these questions truthfully, the recruiter is able to provide the following information, which is pivotal to creating the first level of indoctrination to what will essentially be an ongoing coaching program.

Marine Offer: "Now that you have identified your weaknesses and areas of improvement, let me tell you how the Marines are going to help you strengthen, mold, and improve your character throughout the next years of your life, so that you *can* achieve the goals that are important to you."

Any employer who is studying this will notice a fascinating lesson in the duality of performance in the workplace: High performance is not a one-way street. It is a state created by the raw material of character and talent on the part of the candidate interacting with the raw material of continuous guidance, continuous opportunity, and continuous leadership on the part of the employer.

Another Training Tip for Managers: Give Your People a Writing Assignment

I have mentioned several times in the course of this book that writing ability is inextricably connected to an assessment of potential when looking at the qualities of many managers and team members across industries.

By *writing ability* I don't mean we are looking for Shakespeare or Jane Austen—I am simply referring to the ability to document what one understands about one's job, one's expected results, and what one plans to do about achieving those results.

Writing, in and of itself, is a mirror of the mind, and in many ways, writing exercises allow you to capture aspects of a team member's understanding of your mission and values, which no assessment test alone can ascertain.

You may ask employees in positions of accountability to write a simple SWOT analysis (strengths, weaknesses, opportunities, and threats) about what they perceive to be your company's competitive advantages. Or you may ask them to write a simple essay describing what they feel are the greatest strengths of your company, and the greatest opportunities they have for making a contribution. Or you may ask them to write a short essay on any other mission-related topic of your choice, and then have the quality of these documents graded by an internal leader whose judgment you trust.

Key qualitative points to look for and grade might be:

* **Follow-up:** Did the team member respond to the exercise in a timely fashion?

* **Attitude:** Did he or she display a cooperative, willing, and interested attitude when completing the assignment?

* **Effort:** Did he or she put out a poor, average, or excellent amount of effort?

* **Knowledge:** Did he or she seem to possess a poor, average, or excellent level of knowledge about the company's or department's goals and the effort and skills needed to achieve those goals?

* **Alignment:** Did he or she clearly articulate where he or she fits in, and where he or she sees the greatest opportunities to make a contribution?

* **Self-reliance:** Did he or she display a quality of self-reliance in completing the task, or seek too much help, and rely on others too much?

✖ **Willingness to learn:** Did he or she put forth poor, average, or excellent effort in seeking out resources and learning new information in the process of completing the task?

These are but a few factors that can be studied and measured by the simple assignment of job-related writing exercises. Coupled with the use of other measures, such as assessment tests and the collection of in-house performance data (goal attainment), writing exercises can be invaluable in helping you to truly get a comprehensive picture of a team member's energy, passion, commitment, attitude, and willingness to put out that extra level of mental effort that means so much when analyzing potential.

But perhaps most important is this: Writing exercises can help you ascertain what a team member plans to *do* (what *actions* they plan to take) in the near future in order to step up to the plate and *implement* the goals for which they have been made *accountable*.

Ultimately, what you really want to find out is whether a team member has a knowledge, drive, passion, and concern for your business, and how and why he or she is committed to doing something abut the goals you feel are most important.

When you ask people to put this down on paper, you will usually learn a lot in a short amount of time—about what they know, what they are willing to learn, and how much thought they have already given to the goals that matter to you most.

The Importance of Optimism in Management and Coaching

Not too long ago I was working on a selection and retention analysis problem at a call center in the financial services industry. They were having some major retention problems. People were dropping like flies.

We did a cultural assessment through field interviews and assessments, and found that the top performers who *did* want to stay seemed to possess the following traits:

✕ A desire to interact with many people during the day.

✕ A high degree of need to constantly, verbally communicate with people.

✕ A highly talkative nature and outgoing personality.

✕ Excellent verbal communication skills.

✕ A desire to genuinely help people.

✕ A desire to solve problems for people.

✕ A desire to feel useful in the world.

✕ A desire to do something worthwhile.

✕ The need to have a "workplace family" and a place to belong.

✕ The need to have caring mentors.

✕ The need to be able to prove themselves to someone and themselves.

So, in a combined *skill-based* interview and *motivation-based* interview format we proposed, we suggested that interviewers look for the following traits and indicators among others:

✕ Adaptability.

✕ Energy.

✕ Ability to use computers and telephones with basic skills and confidence.

✕ A talkative, social, outgoing, and confident nature.

✕ A strong desire to prove themselves to someone—hopefully a strong mentoring manager.

✕ A genuine interest in helping people solve their problems.

But looking for a candidate such as that could not possibly solve the entire retention issue, because there was another problem: There were management issues, and in my experience, management issues are the single greatest cause of retention problems.

In our assessment of one manager, we found a rather low score for optimism, bordering on pessimism. So, gently, in our coaching session with the manager, we asked him if he thought he was portraying optimism on the floor with the people he was managing.

"Not really, I guess," the manager said truthfully. "That is something I suppose I need to work on."

A colleague of mine who was in the management coaching session then launched into a speech characteristic of a former football coach:

> But you're their coach! You're everything to them. They watch your every move. They feel the way you feel. They act the way you act. They play the way you play. Don't you want this team to feel like Super Bowl material? The whole thing's on you. You're the nuclear power plant of purpose and passion. No matter what happens, you have to walk in here every day and be the most optimistic human being on the face of the earth, the most enthusiastic person they have ever seen. The coach!

There was a long moment of silence. The manager contemplated this. Then he said, "You're right. You're absolutely right. But I wonder if it will sound phony if I start acting enthusiastic all of a sudden." We emphatically advised the manager that any day is a good day to start acting more enthusiastic around your team members. Enthusiasm hardly ever fails. The time to start being more enthusiastic is now.

Additional Management Class on Retention Strategies

In his book *Peak Performance: Aligning the Hearts and Minds of Your Employees* (Harvard Business School Press, 2000), Jon Katzenbach addresses a realization that many great managers have intuitively known for ages, but may not have precisely documented—the realization that people will have higher levels of performance if they are emotionally committed to their work. In other words, people will be more successful in their jobs if their hearts are in it.

The troubling issue, according to Katzenbach, is that many companies talk about the importance of nurturing employee fulfillment, but not every company has a specific plan for helping their people actually achieve these interrelated goals. Katzenbach conducted research on high-performing workforces at more than 20 leading companies, such as The Home Depot, Southwest Airlines, Avon, Marriott, and even the U.S. Marine Corps. What he found was that companies and organizations that actually have a plan to help people become more emotionally committed and emotionally connected to their work are more competitive than those that don't. It is the emotional commitment to company success that creates a competitive workforce that is able to consistently deliver higher levels of performance than the competition, Katzenbach concludes. In order to develop a strategy for balancing employee fulfillment with organizational performance, Katzenbach purports, the best-performing companies seem to be giving attention to five important areas that he describes as "paths." These paths to success, which enable the cultivation of employee fulfillment and organizational performance, are:

1. The path of building mission, values, and pride.
2. The path of defining business process and performance metrics.

3. The path of cultivating an entrepreneurial spirit.

4. The path of enabling individual achievement.

5. The path of recognizing and celebrating achievement.

Finally, Katzenbach makes the point that in truly competitive organizations, leaders recognize that it is important to balance emotional fulfillment in employees with organizational success, and to actually do something on a regular basis to make sure that important areas such as the five paths of success outlined here are given more than lip service.

As a great manager who is concerned about keeping your best people, you probably want to make a few field notes here as well:

Examine those five paths and write notes on what you have done to accentuate those paths lately. What would you like to do?

Basic Principles for Increasing Incentive

When seeking to assess and develop teams, continuous assessment, coaching, and training is key. High performers like to know there they stand, and where they need the most help in order to improve their performance.

Finally, here are a few points to use as guideposts when seeking to increase the retention of your high-performing team members.

Critical Steps for Retaining High–Performing Individuals

+ Always be fair in setting expectations.

+ Use multiple avenues of assessment to get a well-rounded view of performance and development needs.

+ Analyze assessment data in the context of existing training—have team members been given the right resources and a fair chance to learn so far?

+ Discuss assessment data as a management team—decide what additional training and resources need to be provided.

+ Factor in morale issues—are there poor managers or other factors that may be contributing to poor performance?

+ Give meaningful but challenging tasks to gauge the team member's degree of individual initiative and self-reliance.

+ Use written exercises and verbal presentations before a group as part of the learning process.

+ Making training and coaching individualized wherever possible.

+ Make sure your selection process is highly specific in identifying the types of individuals who will succeed on your team in the first place.

In the next chapter, we will be given additional examples from multiple industries to show how the use of validated and competency-based selection tools can help in your efforts to be more successful in hiring high-performing individuals. This chapter will also continue to demonstrate why peak performance is always achieved when great people are being led by great managers. Thus, we will continue to discuss why there must always be consistency between the skills and competencies of your selected team members and the managers who have been hired to guide and educate them.

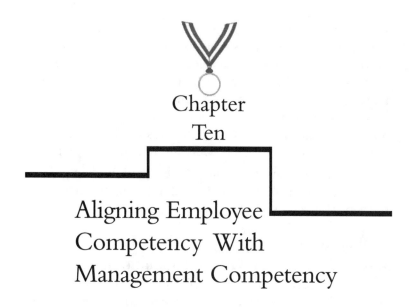

Chapter Ten

Aligning Employee Competency With Management Competency

The very practice of incorporating competency-based assessment as part of an overall selection and development strategy implies that different jobs require different competencies. In this chapter we will show the way the use of existing competency models constructed by industrial psychologists who study performance trends may be of help to you as you seek to continue streamlining your selection and development process. As we will also discuss, it is essential to study the competencies of team members along with an assessment of the managers who are guiding them. This is essential for uncovering potential communication or coaching problems that may be standing in the way of team morale and productivity.

Competency Model Example One: Healthcare

We will use the healthcare industry as a primary example in this section for several reasons. The first reason is that I have experience as a consultant to the healthcare industry, so I have practical field notes stemming from that experience that corroborate the evidence following. The second reason is that the healthcare field offers classic examples of a career environment that puts tremendous amounts of stress on almost all employees and managers. Any tools and strategies that can help improve morale and retention in the pressure-cooker environment of healthcare service delivery are bound to help others.

Having said that, let us now take a look at some of the specific competencies that are known to be important areas of assessment in a cross-section of occupations.

Healthcare Service Competencies: Maintaining a Service Mentality in Grueling Conditions

In this section and others, I will draw upon personal experience and field notes, coupled with the research done by David Bigby, PhD, and his associates. Their research has meticulously outlined the skills, competencies, and traits that are known to be predictors of success in the jobs we will examine in this chapter.

The data on these competencies was supplied by my partners at the Omaha-based assessment and consulting firm VantagePoint, Inc., led by Jeff West. The validated findings discussed here are drawn from predictive tools used by VantagePoint with a wide range of customers.

Through extensive research within the healthcare industry (hospitals, clinics, home health, and other environments) it has been demonstrated that success in many of the high-stress jobs in healthcare require that you select people who remain composed under pressure, have a service orientation toward patients, and are cooperative with family members and other staff. Selecting employees that exhibit these traits (above and beyond having the skills and knowledge necessary to do the job) has proven to result in hires that perform better, are evaluated more favorably by colleagues, and are likely to stay in the position for longer periods of time.

For service-oriented positions, the assessment of these traits can help you identify service personnel in healthcare who have the resilience, positive attitude, and work ethic that will enable them to consistently maintain a strong service attitude even in the face of high stress, a relentless work schedule, and multiple demands.

However, as we have discussed at length in this book, careful selection involves the use of a multiphased process, and the use of several tools in order select people who have a bona fide track record of commitment, diligence, and integrity in their careers.

That is especially true when selecting executives or key practitioners in the heathcare industry, the biotech industry, and the pharmaceutical industry.

In the next section, my colleague Peter C. Johnson, MD, CEO of the Raleigh, North Carolina–based biotech consulting firm Scintellix, who also heads up the biotech recruiting division of Headway, will share his observations on the additional skills and competencies he finds important to study and assess when selecting high-performing executives or practitioners in the healthcare, biotech, and pharmaceutical fields. Dr. Johnson's insights add an interesting philosophical dimension to the competencies I have discussed. Perhaps most intriguing is his observation that executives in life sciences and healthcare must be profoundly open-minded and lacking in any form of professional cynicism.

♛ ♛ ♛

Special Competencies of Senior Leaders in Biotechnology, Pharmaceuticals, and Healthcare
by Peter C. Johnson, MD

The choice of a senior leader in biotechnology/pharmaceutical companies and healthcare institutions casts a long shadow on the future progress of each of these institutions. The business venture in each case is imbued with a high degree of hopefulness and a dearth of predictability. Whether it be the early or late development of a drug or the care of a major hospital system, unpredictables are the order of the day. As a consequence, executives in these sectors must have the ability to create believable visions from what are essentially hopeful prospects.

This requires confidence. However, successful leaders in these areas do not express blind confidence. Rather, they collect data continuously from their personnel, and resolve from the data the most highly probable course of success—and then convey a reasonable confidence in that course. In effect, they are saying to their organization that no matter what the outcome of our next step, we will be able to take in all new data and re-resolve the situation, correct our course, and keep moving forward. Much like a vehicle's Global Positioning System, when a wrong turn is made, a new course is computed instantly.

Excellent executives have an ongoing creative drive to resolve incomplete data so that a compelling and meaningful business story can be conveyed to their staff and to the external world. They are not daunted by having been on a temporarily errant course. Their joy lies in continuously reassessing progress to drive ever closer to their goals.

A critical personal feature that makes this approach successful is the capacity to avoid cynicism in their own work and to expect the same from those around them. In order to resolve course data with the greatest degree of accuracy, they need to keep all degrees of freedom open. Cynicism quietly but firmly poisons this process. An active war on cynicism by the chief executive is felt throughout the organization as an openness to ideas, a sense of fairness and good judgment, and the desire to create the future with a sense of pleasure. When this is missing, a series of events occurs that leads to the perception of "preferred" to "non-preferred" employees, to the creation of cliques, to the withholding of information and ideas, and, ultimately, a restriction of corporate progress.

There are many skills necessary to be a successful chief executive in the life sciences and healthcare. Each of these businesses lives at the "edge of science," where things—especially biological cause and effect—may not yet be wholly known. They consequently exhibit greater uncertainties than most businesses. This creates demands on chief executives that are unique in their intensity. The successful executive realizes that his or her prime function is to process all incoming information so as to reduce uncertainty in the business and to convey new plateaus in understanding to all stakeholders, continuously. In order to gain access to the maximum amount of information that is needed to form sound judgments, such executives must display an openness to information from all quarters, a posture that is best achieved by caring deeply about one's employees and the noble purpose being pursued by the company. All else follows from this.

Call Center Selection: How Productivity Is Affected by Selection and Management

One of the most interesting—and important—career choices today that should involve great scrutiny on the part of the employer is call center employment.

As stated in previous chapters, hiring call center professionals is a critical task for many companies, because the customer service delivery and aptitude of call center workers is directly linked to many important factors, such as customer satisfaction, customer retention, future sales, and corporate image.

Just as we have discussed in previous chapters, there is a strong link between the performance of call center professionals and the aptitude of their managers, which also can and should be addressed. In fact, in some of the call centers I have worked with, executives have attributed a significant amount of attrition and poor performance to poor management, which ultimately has to be traced back to poor management selection.

The skills and attributes that predict success in call center professions differ according to the particular type of call center job—inbound service, inbound sales, outbound sales, help desk, and so on. In looking at predictive assessments of a call center professional in a particular job (and this holds true for numerous other jobs as well), you should evaluate both capability to do the job (measurement of the innate characteristics that lead to success in the role) and willingness to do it (measurement of work ethic, or a positive outlook on working hard and earning one's pay). Key dimensions of innate capability to do the job that often lead to success in outbound sales roles include frustration tolerance (ability to bounce back from disappointments), ability to influence others, and a strong sense of accountability (preference for having one's performance monitored). For help-desk agents, some of the same attributes predict performance, but there are other key success factors that are critical in addition to the ones already cited for success in a help-desk environment. These include a preference for solving problems and a willingness to collaborate with others to achieve successful problem resolution.

Additional Traits Required of Call Center Managers

As we have discussed many times in this book, and will discuss even more, managers who build, grow, and sustain successful teams must have all of the traits required of the people they manage, plus a series of other traits that will allow them to earn the trust of and then educate the people under their watch and care.

For call center managers, a general supervisor competency model would in some cases be helpful. Such a general model would include the following profile. (These competencies, which can be scientifically measured, are important for many other management jobs as well. As you examine this list, try to think where you might score on all of these core management competencies. Is there anything you would like to improve on this list that might make you a better manager to your people? Are there any managers on your team who might be lacking in any of these areas?)

- ✦ **Decisive Judgment**—Making good decisions in a timely and confident manner.

- ✦ **Adapting to Change**—Adapting to changing situations, and restructuring tasks and priorities as changes occur within the business and organization.

- ✦ **Planning and Organizing**—Effectively organizing and planning work according to organizational needs by defining objectives and anticipating needs and priorities.

- ✦ **Driving for Results**—Challenging, pushing the organization and themselves to excel and achieve.

- ✦ **Managing Others**—Directing and leading others to accomplish organizational goals and objectives.

- ✦ **Coaching and Development of Others**—Advising, assisting, mentoring, and providing feedback to others to encourage and inspire the development of work-related competencies and long-term career growth.

- ✦ **Motivating Others**—Inspiring others to perform well by actively conveying enthusiasm and a passion for doing a good job.

- ✦ **Functional Acumen**—Having the skills, knowledge, and abilities necessary to be effective in the specific function of a job.

- ✦ **Integrity**—Upholding a high standard of fairness and ethics in everyday words and actions.

(Wording on these traits supplied by ASSESS Systems.)

All of these traits, many of which are necessary for other management positions as well, combine to help a person be a better educator, mentor, and coach.

Common Barriers to Productivity at Call Centers

Following are common comments that are made by professionals in different levels of the organization when asked about lack of productivity in call centers.

It is important to study the common complaints of *all* employee levels when facing productivity issues. As you can tell from the following examples, the common denominator in virtually all complaints at all levels is "lack of adequate communication between departments."

Common Executive Observations at Call Centers

Often, a key observation of the executive team at call centers is that there is substantial room for improvement in the overall process guiding the selection, assessment, and development of managers. It is widely recognized that management skills, or lack thereof, often has a significant effect on retention. Most executives also see room for improvement in the selection, assessment, or development of agents or customer care representatives. It is also recognized that selection efforts must do a better job of analyzing the specific traits necessary for success in different types of call center jobs. For instance, some jobs may require sales skills, while others may require advanced technical knowledge. In general, many executives acknowledge that the lack of a formalized recruitment and development process often creates enormous operational, staffing, and revenue attainment problems at every level of the company's business platform, especially with regard to retention and productivity.

Here is what some call center operations managers say are the most important traits for call center managers to have, in terms of their relationships with agents.

✦ Managers will defend agents, and "have their back."

✦ Managers will be approachable, and also approach their team members.

✦ Managers will be loyal, compassionate, honest, courageous, and reliable.

✦ Managers will be interested in their team members' success.

✦ Managers will be invested (and demonstrate that fact) in their team members' success.

✦ Managers will be innovative and will teach and foster innovation.

✦ Managers will be self-examining.

✦ Managers will show excellent follow-through.

When agents themselves asked why productivity is low, they typically mention four key factors:

1. Low pay.
2. Inconsistent hiring (they are forced to work with low achievers, and this weakens morale).
3. Inconsistent management (this further erodes morale).
4. Lack of adequate training.

Do any of those issues affect your organization too? If so, what can you do about it?

Lack of Confidence Issues

In one case we studied, the widespread lack of confidence among agents was attributable to three factors:

1. Lack of training.
2. Lack of coaching.
3. Lack of knowing whether anyone cares about them.

What Managers and Agents Agree on in Hiring

Interestingly, both managers and agents for call centers often agree that the following traits are important for agents, and even some agents feel their managers should do a better job in hiring people with these traits:

- Call center agent candidates should have demonstrated a high degree of dedication to something in the past.

- Call center agent candidates should demonstrate a high degree of aptitude for paying attention.

- Call center agent candidates should demonstrate a high degree of willingness and eagerness to learn.

- Call center agent candidates should demonstrate problem-solving skills and an interest in solving new problems.

- Call center agent candidates should find difficult people interesting as a challenge to overcome.

- Call center agent candidates should like making new connections with people of all types.

- Call center agent candidates should be extremely flexible and able to adapt to different buying types.

- Call center agent candidates should be able to understand both the technical needs and ego needs of all customers.

- Call center agent candidates should have a good answer when asked why they want the job—not just "my mom wants me to have a job."

Guiding Principles for Superior Management and Higher Retention

In light of the following examples, and the call center productivity observations made by executives, managers, and agents alike, it seems clear that the following principles are clear guidelines for call center leadership in all seasons.

These principles transcend race, ethnicity, or gender. They are simply the principles that all high achievers seem to respond to best, in the face of all challenges.

- ✦ Always set high expectations.
- ✦ Always be fair.
- ✦ Always reward excellence.
- ✦ Never show favoritism.
- ✦ Teach, teach, teach, and teach some more.
- ✦ Always set the example.
- ✦ Always be seen as the most helpful person your employees have ever met.

The steady and relentless execution of the management principles, in most instances, should go a long way to helping improve productivity at most, if not all, call centers, based on validated research of call center management competency and our own exhaustive interviews in the field. They are also key guidelines for successful management in most other organizations as well.

In the following section, I will share a story about the critical importance of mentoring in all organizations. It occurs at a memorable dinner I shared with a national leader in the banking industry.

A Deeper View of Mentoring: Tips From a Man Who Should Know

Once every 10 years or so, you hear a statement from a business leader that seems to throw a powerful light of truth and common sense on all of those small and sensible things that each one of us can do as individuals to make the organizations we work for better. One of those statements that I find impossible to forget came one evening when I met with Frank Skillern, the former CEO of American Express Centurion Bank.

"In 40 years of leadership I have basically learned one thing, and it is the most important thing I know," Mr. Skillern said. "Companies really only perform when every team member knows that there is at least one person there who sincerely cares what happens to them in their career. That's where it all begins and ends. That, in my view, is the single truth that drives success."

As we consider the enormous challenges all of us face in seeking to hire, retain, and *inspire* committed and customer-focused team members in our organizations, it is critical that we never forget the simplicity of Mr. Skillern's observation. His poignant reminder, which speaks to mentoring, strikes to the very heart of retention and morale issues at most organizations, where job stress is often high.

The crisis that many organizations face is this: No matter how much time and energy you spend on selecting great people, it only takes one bad manager to drive them out the door as fast as you can bring them in. Others have covered this subject matter in elaborate detail. Research by the Gallup Organization and books such as *First Break All the Rules* by Curt Coffman and Marcus Buckingham (which is based on the Gallup research), essentially show that team members don't leave organizations—they leave bad managers.

In this light, Mr. Skillern's observation about the importance of mentoring suggests that we can take a *proactive* response in management by making sure that some semblance of a mentoring program is in place in every corner of our organizations. Can we say with certainty that every person who works with us knows that there is at least one other person within the building who genuinely cares about their career? If not, then why not? And isn't that a relatively easy thing to work on? In this light it may not suffice to merely say that people leave companies because of bad management.

They could just as easily be leaving because they see no signs of mentoring.

It is easy to be overwhelmed when you think of all the tasks required to build sweeping leadership, management development, and employee training programs. But the first and most important point of change could be simple.

Why not simply implement a mentoring program, in which you pair every single employee with one peer professional whose task it is to mentor greatness, passion, and professionalism, and to communicate daily to their colleague how much they genuinely care what happens to them in their career—and then help them succeed?

If this and only this were done in most organizations, we could virtually guarantee that more people would be showing up for work earlier, with less complaints, and more zeal for the job.

As we have demonstrated in this chapter, the use of industry-specific, validated, and competency-based assessment and selection tools can help you do a much better job in selecting top performers.

However, it is always critical to keep in mind that it is virtually impossible to retain top performers if you do not carefully select managers whom those high performers will respect. In order for that relationship of trust between the employee and manager to exist, as we have demonstrated, the manager must have all of the traits, skills, and competencies the high performer is expected to have—plus additional traits that allow the manager to motivate, lead by example, and educate.

In the next chapter, we turn our attention to the complex but fascinating challenge of selecting top managers and executives. The observations made in the next chapter come from research on the psychology of leadership that I have used and participated in while studying effective leaders at hundreds of companies throughout the past 20 years.

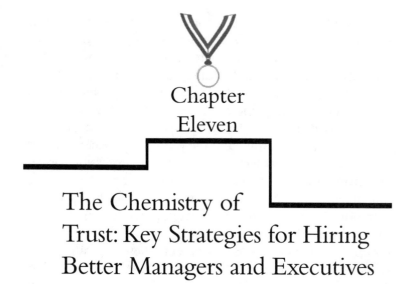

Chapter
Eleven

The Chemistry of Trust: Key Strategies for Hiring Better Managers and Executives

With regard to excellence, it is not enough to know, but we must try to have and use it.

—Aristotle

In looking at the leadership qualities and styles that are most important for both executives and managers, four traits seem to be critical.

We will call these traits the **four factors of integrity**—and by *integrity* we mean wholeness, or completeness. Understanding that "wholeness" is a critical ingredient of leadership is key. To express it another way, great leaders possess a constellation of powerful traits that are woven and integrated throughout their being. As authors Robert and Carolyn Turknett put it in their book *Decent People/Decent Company: How to Lead with Character at Work and in Life* (Davies-Black, 2005), "Character is who you are at the core of your being." As the authors also state, "Integrity is the fundamental quality of character: knowing your values, and being true to them at any cost." Sometimes people ask what *integrity* really means. One way to view integrity is to understand that integrity is not just honesty; integrity has much to do with *integration*—a complete integration of one's values to the extent that those values will not be compromised, neither at home nor in the workplace. As I have studied executives throughout the years, it has become apparent that the building blocks of integrity and professional excellence can actually be broken down into four factors: character, functional competence, commitment, and vision. As we will demonstrate, the overarching portrait of an executive's integrity is revealed by his or her track record in all of these areas. For this reason I have chosen to refer to these separate dimensions as the four factors of integrity. These four dimensions seem to define the most important characteristics of successful executives—those who are able to manage successfully and lead successfully at the same time.

1. **Character Integrity.** Does the executive possess those critical traits of character, such as self-reliance, diligence, honesty, appreciation of others, and a desire to prove one's worth, that you are also striving to select in your non-managerial team members? Does the manager both exemplify and model those traits for others, leading by example? The examination of soft skills such as communication expertise and emotional intelligence would be studied as part of a character integrity probe.

2. **Functional Integrity.** Does the executive possess the hard skills that would be required of others on a high-performing team that the executive would be asked to manage? In other words, will the team members trust that the executive is an expert in the functional areas they are supposed to have mastered? Most importantly, can the executive *teach*? If the executive were to teach his or her team members to

be better in some way, what would he or she teach? And what would make him or her qualified to teach? What are his or her teaching credentials? In many cases, the possession of character integrity and functional integrity is more important than specific industry experience. An executive with strong character who has proved him- or herself to be an excellent teacher is also very teachable. Leaders who have not proven themselves as teachers usually are not very teachable, regardless of their industry experience. They have a low passion for learning and growing.

3. **Commitment Integrity.** Can the executive clearly articulate his or her areas of talent? Can the executive also clearly demonstrate in writing how he or she has done his or her best to use those talents to the fullest in the workplace? Looking at this written record, do you get a portrait of a person who knows that time is precious, that talent is precious, and who did not want to waste a second of either time or talent? Executives who write about their histories with vague terms, handy leadership buzzwords, and all the latest trendy things to say, may have lived a life without much purpose. They may have been relying on the thoughts of others, instead of making the most of their own thoughts. Commitment integrity is a barometer of passion and purpose. When people with commitment integrity talk or write about their histories, you can see the struggle, you can see the challenges, you can see them pushing their way to the finish line, covered in blood and sweat. Those are the people you want to keep cheering on. They are also the people you want to hire. Better to be cheering for them on your team than someone else's.

4. **Vision Integrity.** Does the executive understand where he or she wants to improve his or her own performance, both for personal reasons and for the good of the team and the company? Great leaders understand both their strengths

and weaknesses, and realize that no organizations will raise the bar unless individuals are dedicated to raising the bar within themselves. They never rest on their laurels. By being ruthlessly honest with themselves, and dedicated to improvement, they inspire others to do so. When they talk to others about the need for raising the bar, others trust them, because they know the leader holds him- or herself just as accountable, or more accountable, than he or she holds others. This vision and integrity, combined with character integrity, functional integrity, and commitment integrity creates the chemistry of trust within all high-performing organizations and high-performing teams.

Subsequent portions of this chapter will demonstrate specific tools and strategies you can use to analyze or measure these important areas of integrity in your executive hires by using a multiphased approach to assessment and interviewing.

But first, let us consider a few anecdotes, examples, and case histories from the real world that show the kind of chaos and confusion that can occur if you do not focus on these areas of integrity in your hiring or promotion process.

One of the most humorous but enlightening stories I have ever heard about problematic executive hires came from the lips of a good friend of mine, who has served as a marketing consultant to several CEOs in New York.

What follows is a true story. You may be stunned to hear that this is a true story—or maybe not. At any rate, I believe this story operates as a perfect parable on the challenges of making good executive hires—and the deadly consequences of making poor ones. The theme, or moral of this story, is simple— you must hire and promote executives who have not lost the "common touch," as Rudyard Kipling would say, and who also possess a humble, detailed, and craftsman-like approach to their area of expertise. These are the only kind of managers that team members trust. Now here's the story to explain that principle.

Several years ago, my friend was contacted by the CEO of one of the largest banks in the world, who wanted an outside consultant to study his marketing department, because he felt his top executives were displaying a lack of ingenuity. So, because my friend has received a lot of press as a marketing guru in New York, the CEO asked her if she would come in and ask his four top marketing executives a series of questions. Among other things, he wanted to hear what each one thought were the top four marketing messages of the corporation, just to see if everyone was on the same page.

So, that same week, my friend made appointments with the top four marketing executives. When she showed up for those meetings and asked the question about the four top marketing messages, she was astounded by what she heard.

In each case, the marketing executives told her that they did not know what the four top marketing messages were, because that wasn't their job. Each one used slightly different wording, but in essence they all said the same thing: "That is not my job. My job is to look at the big picture."

Now, I know some of you are laughing and can't believe this is true, but it *is* true. Let's take a look at what happened next.

The following week, my friend went back in to see the CEO of this large bank (again, one of the largest banks in the world).

"Did you ask them what they thought the four top messages of this company are?" the CEO asked.

"Yes," my friend replied.

"And what did they say?"

"They said they didn't know. They also said that it was not their job, because their job is to look at the big picture," she said.

"I see," the CEO replied. "Well, you did a good job. That is about all I need." The meeting lasted five minutes.

That afternoon, an executive search firm received an order for four executive marketing positions.

This one simple story encapsulates many of the challenges that are created when you choose form over substance in making executive or managerial hires. Clearly, the marketing executives described, whether they had been promoted from the inside or hired from the outside, had done a good job of convincing someone that they were management material. Maybe these executives had charisma; perhaps they were good networkers, talked a good game, were great at having other people do the real work for them. Perhaps they were simply adept at climbing the corporate ladder. But for whatever reason, it was also clear that all of them had forgotten one basic principle of good executive leadership: It is never wise to become so aloof that you stray too far from the knitting, as the old saying goes. That, in essence, is the key difficulty in hiring or promoting executives and managers. Because executives and managers are capable of delegating, they can often disguise their ineptitude by getting other people to do their work for them. When executives and managers submit resumes, furthermore, numbers cited for productivity and performance can be confounding. You may have a hard time getting anyone to tell you if the performance was actually the result of the manager's own talent and critical thinking abilities, or whether it was the result of some unsung hero who never got credit for anything.

Because of this, it is just as important to put executive and managerial hires through the same kind of multiphased hiring process that you would demand of team members reporting to them.

Before we move on to a few relevant case histories that help explain best practices in executive hiring, let me pause to point out what I feel are a few important action points for hiring better executives. I will intersperse throughout this chapter a series of such action points. These points are tied to the principles we cited in the chapter on creating a multiphased selection process for key team members.

✦ Make sure that you do not hire executives who think their primary job is to look at the big picture, and who think the "small stuff" is beneath them. Such an attitude usually describes a mixture of arrogance and laziness. A great executive should be your greatest subject matter expert and the hardest worker on the team.

✦ Use validated competencies as part of the process to get a benchmark for organizational aptitude, critical thinking abilities, analytical skills, insight, decisive judgment, self-reliance, fact-based thinking, attitude toward people, and other characteristics and competencies you know are important to the job.

✦ Make sure you put your executive hires through as many hoops as possible before you hire them. Be demanding. Force them to show you how self-reliant and dedicated they are. Make it hard to get the job. Don't focus on their polish—see how much work they are willing to do. If at any point the candidate suggests you are asking too much of him or her in the hiring process, pounce on it. You just found yourself a streak of entitlement.

✦ Force your executive candidates to write something about their values and their successes. Make the assignment hard. Make it clear that they should do the exercise themselves and not have someone else complete it for them. You don't want to hire people who are used to leaning on others for everything and barking out orders. You want people who can think and work for themselves. And if an executive cannot articulate in writing the essence of his or her character and how it has been inextricably linked to their specific business successes, you probably want to cancel the interview and move on.

Executive Character Reflects a History of Discipline

In an essay originally published in the *Harvard Business Review* (March–April, 1998) titled "The Discipline of Building Character," based on his book *Defining Moments: When Managers Must Choose Between Right and Right* (Harvard Business School Press, 1997), Joseph L. Badaracco, Jr., speaks of "defining moments" that help us understand what great executives are truly made of.

Defining moments occur when tough challenges force great executives to make tough decisions for the good of the company. But the thing that separates great executives from mediocre executives is this: The great ones remember those moments vividly. As the author states, "To become leaders, managers need to translate their personal values into *calculated* action." (Emphasis mine.) Executives who successfully resolve defining moments, according to Badarraco, are "able to dig below the busy surface of their daily lives and refocus on their core values and principles. Once uncovered, those values and principles renew their sense of purpose at work and act as a springboard for shrewd, pragmatic, politically astute action."

The history of translating values into action in challenging circumstances is in line with the thinking of a great educator from days gone by, Aristotle, who also emphasized the importance of action as a defining principle of leadership. As he astutely stated: "With regard to excellence, it is not enough to know, but we must try to have and use it."

Therefore, a good question to pose to any executive worth his or her salt would be as follows:

Question: Tell me about a defining moment in your career, a point in which you had to make a tough decision, and all of your strengths of integrity came into play—your character, your functional knowledge and teaching ability, your commitment to a set of values, and your vision of how business could be improved. What was the situation, what made it challenging, and what exactly did you do? And how did all of the areas of integrity we just mentioned enable you to be successful?

Champion managers and executives will usually be able to give you a detailed description of such pivotal defining moments, and you will hear (or see) passion in their words when they speak or write about these defining moments, because they have lived them and learned from them.

Mediocre managers usually won't have much to say, or their words will be so vague and rambling that you won't be able to follow them. You will not be inspired at the end of the discussion, and you will find yourself not having learned much.

Creating Character–Centered Job Descriptions for Executive Positions and Postings

One key to attracting and sourcing great managerial talent is to write very specific and clear job descriptions that emphasize the type of culture you have and what you expect.

For starters, you want to make sure you eliminate people who are looking for a "comfortable" place to work. I cannot tell you how many times I have interviewed candidates about their interest in a company, and heard phrases such as, "This is a place where I could feel very comfortable." Such a response, if it is a person's first response, makes *me* feel a little *un*comfortable. It makes me think that their first order of business, if hired, will be to move in a comfy sofa, upon which they can nap in the middle of the afternoon. For managers, I am not looking for someone who is seeking comfort or security—I am looking for someone who would be constantly afraid of underperforming, someone who would always be slightly uncomfortable, and thus furiously driven to prove himself.

So, when writing job descriptions, make sure you point out how difficult the job will be, how challenging, and how relentlessly people will be held accountable for their actions and numbers. Make it clear that if the person is not ready to live in a constant state of high expectations, he or she should not apply. Make sure they know that their background for excellence will also be ruthlessly examined. That should weed out the first hundred worthless interviews.

For the rest of those potential candidates who make it through the door, you want to make sure that they—and your hiring managers—are absolutely clear on the expectations of the job and the character traits the company is looking for.

Before sending out any postings, make sure that you have examined the heart of the job from the same simple vantage point that we outlined in the first chapter. In this case, however, where leaders are concerned, you are attempting to analyze the necessary skills that the employee will need in order to both *implement* the job and *teach* the job to others under his or her leadership.

What follows is a version of the job description worksheet and planning tool offered in an earlier chapter, slightly modified for analyzing executive positions.

In defining the heart of the job for this executive, I am looking for a person who will lead by example in displaying the following three key traits (add more traits if you feel they are necessary):

1. _____

2. _____

3. _____

(Just as we discussed in the first chapter, it is critical to think carefully about these items. In order to do these things with excellence, a person must want to prove something to you, or show you, every day, that his or her heart is in it. Remember that before you fill in the blanks above. What is being proved to you and your customers by the items you just defined?)

Other Key Skills I Need From the Executive:

(In order for them to lead by example. Can they teach these skills?)

1. _____

2. _____

3. _____

Key Experiences and Background I Need:

1. _____

2. _____

3. _____

You are taking all of these initial steps in analyzing the job in order to find those people who possess what I would like to call the essential qualities that build trust in teams. These are executives who naturally assume that their job is to play the servant's role, to work harder than anyone else on the team, to help with the heavy lifting, to prove themselves every day, to hold themselves to higher standards of account-ability than those they manage, to strive endlessly to help others, and to constantly set the example.

With these thoughts in mind, let's move on to a case history that will demonstrate the relevance of character modeling and selection throughout the fabric of an organization.

A Committed Strategy in Character–Based Selection

In 2003, Headway Corporate Resources filed for bank-ruptcy protection, largely because revenue could not keep pace with debt service requirements. At the request of the board, Jean-Pierre (J.P.) Sakey, an investment banker who had most recently helped run North America for Monster.com, was asked to examine the corporation and provide a forensic ac-counting analysis of the company's woes. Key goals were to establish a sense of whether Headway was still viable as a company, and if so, what needed to be done to create a better image and brand for the company, and what needed to be done to bring debt under control, escalate sales, define better niches, and create profits. As a result of Sakey's report to the board, upper management was replaced, and Sakey was asked by the board to come in as president and CEO. During the earlier stages of the rebuilding, Sakey asked me to collabo-rate with him on improving recruiting models and strategies that would serve as a gold standard for the industry, and to assemble a "best and brightest team" of consultants and ex-perts who would help us do that.

In analyzing all of the current best practices and strategies in recruiting, and the best assessment tools and practices, it began to dawn on us that *character* was an element essential to any company's success, and that most companies—even recruiting companies—were not spending enough time probing candidates' track records of character. Furthermore, discussions about the problems Headway had faced in the past—problems that had led it to bankruptcy—and the problems faced by many other companies, in many cases boiled down to a problem of entitlement. Executives and team members who feel entitled do not view their primary job as one of servanthood or stewardship—they are under the impression that others are primarily there to serve them and their interests.

In looking at some of the problems of entitlement that may have plagued Headway in the past, Sakey decided to create a working environment that would eradicate entitlement at every level possible. The goal was to create a culture of stewardship, in which everyone, no matter how elevated their position, was expected to play the servant's role. We hope the next example will demonstrate the way relatively simple and clear signs can help you determine whether key executives possess an attitude of entitlement or an attitude of stewardship.

Cultures of Entitlement vs. Cultures of Stewardship

One interesting and telling story I heard about the culture of Headway prior to the change in management came from the mouth of a former executive. This executive mentioned that on several occasions other executives had asked him to play the part of a chauffer for them, and that they would sit in the back seat of his car talking on their cell phones while he sat alone up front and escorted them to meetings. This executive said that the experience always made him feel uncomfortable.

I find there to be a compelling contrast between this type of culture—such that some executives are asked to play the servant role to *other* executives—and the current culture of the company, such that top executives are expected to be servants to those *beneath* them. A classic example of this is demonstrated by the actions of the CEO himself—Sakey. Although Headway has moved its corporate offices from New York City to Raleigh, North Carolina, it still maintains a New York office for New York business. In this office, the CEO has assigned himself to a cubicle in the middle of the sales force, while giving the larger offices to others. This action seems metaphorical in terms of stewardship.

To reinforce this culture of stewardship, the CEO has stated many times that his role is to help and to serve, and to set an example of what stewardship means. The CEO has also set himself up in the role of teacher—among other duties. I know this personally, because he has spent a great deal of time teaching me. In addition to receiving an education from the CEO on what he has learned about best practices in recruiting throughout the span of his career, I have also received some high-level instruction on forensic business analysis and the nature of profitable businesses. In one memorable meeting, I remember that Sakey attempted to make it simple for me and offered the following insight: "Let me boil it down for you," he said. "Businesses go bankrupt because they don't understand their costs. Keep that thought in your head at all times."

In Headway's new culture, the measure of performance for executives is largely based on character—all of those traits one can see in the actions of others on a daily basis. How self-reliant is an executive? Does an executive lean on others too heavily? Is an executive good at both managing and leading (management referring to the successful implementation of existing goals, and leadership referring to the steady and well-planned creation of new approaches and ideas)? Is that manager seen as someone who is consistently helpful? Do the manager's team members seem to like and respect him or her, in terms of work ethic and treatment of others? Does the manager embody and exemplify the traits the corporation wants its team members to display?

Because the forensic analysis of Headway's problems before the management change so clearly indicated a need to focus on business character first and foremost, it was decided to mobilize the corporation's resources to focus on character-based selection as a recruiting philosophy and process, as well as a means of restructuring Headway's own team. Thus, character-based selection became the company's mission statement and a central part of its internal restructuring plan at the same time. The end result was that the company is now experiencing profitability and growth.

The next section comprises an interview with Sakey, who will explain how Headway was rebuilt, and how an intense focus on leadership character and character assessment was a part of that. The interview will also outline how a more thorough review of the character and track record of executive or managerial candidates is critical to building more successful teams.

Character-Based Teams as a Business Model: An Interview With J.P. Sakey, CEO, Headway Corporate Resources

Snyder: As a result of your forensic analysis, did you detect any character issues at Headway that may have led to some of the company's problems, when the board of directors asked you to help turn Headway around?

Sakey: That's a big question. Let me break it up into parts. First, Headway's problems were evident long before they went into bankruptcy. They went into bankruptcy in the summer of 2003. But these things just don't happen overnight. I was brought in to help engineer Headway out of bankruptcy. During the bankruptcy process, the shareholders of Headway had lost millions of dollars, because debt could not be repaid. The lenders asked me to help because they were afraid that even if Headway was restructured, it was going to be the same old Headway that got them into bankruptcy in the first place.

Snyder: What would characterize it as the same old Headway?

Sakey: I can only tell you what I saw when I got there. From my understanding, what the lender's group saw were unattainable business plans [such that] there was no support to those business plans, and no real change in the business strategy. The business leaders who got the company into trouble simply felt the company had too much debt. They didn't feel like the company had done anything wrong. They didn't feel there was any need to change anything within the company.

Snyder: Obviously something did need to be changed. What did you see? What were the most basic changes that needed to be made?

Sakey: Basically, in looking at the previous leaders, I found a real detachment from the business. In my opinion, they were not personally invested in the business, and they were not personally invested in the people. I saw a sense of angst, and a lot of woe is me, but I didn't see anyone in a leadership role rolling up their shirt sleeves and going to work to fix things—anything to create a new vision, a new purpose, a new way of addressing the marketplace. Also, among the employees, I saw a very low morale, a lot of uncertainty, poor communication everywhere, people not knowing what was going on, not knowing whether they were going to get paid, and working in relatively dingy offices. There seemed to be a general widespread fear of the instability of the company. It kind of reminded me of visiting a dysfunctional family with an abusive past, where everyone is nervous and skittish. That's what it looked like. I saw a very poor self-image everywhere. So, if a company can personify certain behaviors, and personify poor self-image, then it will also personify a lack of self-confidence among employees and a lack of confidence in the marketplace as well. That what was happening. That lack of morale and self-confidence permeated everything and kept the company from having even a chance of being competitive.

Snyder: So what did you first set out to change?

Sakey: Everything. Essentially, I set out to help people regain a sense of self esteem and confidence in themselves, knowing that this would help Headway become a more self-confident organization as a whole. I started with completely refurbishing the offices, and putting a fresh coat of paint on the walls everywhere. This was metaphorical, but important. Second, I let them know that I had a vision for greatness that was based on commitment and character. I wasn't there just to straighten out the debt. I was there to help build a great company.

Snyder: Tell us more about that.

Sakey: When the new owners asked me to step in, I asked them how committed they were to building a great new company. If the bankruptcy group had said to me—now we simply want to polish this up and sell it, or slice this up and sell it, I would have said I'm not interested. But what the board said to me was, we want to build a great company. I said, okay, but if you want to do that, we have to do a number of things.

Snyder: What were those things?

Sakey: Some were highly technical, and involved fixing the balance sheet, committing to a working capital line of credit, committing to business statements we would live by. I told them that if they did what I asked, I would treat the business as if I were in it for life, and become totally invested in the success of Headway. They said okay, and I moved to New York, leaving my home of 25 years in Pittsburgh, and became deeply involved in the business.

Snyder: What was your strategy?

Sakey: Our strategy was two-pronged. The first thing we asked was, what can we do with the business? What can we change to make it more successful? In other words, what can we do about the way we do business to improve overall business? This involved a careful scrutiny of our business lines. This was no small matter, because we have employees and offices all over the United States. In this path, we set about to fix Headway scientifically, if you will, one step at a time, paying attention to every financial detail. On the second path—which was a simultaneous path—we set about to improve the self-image of the company, to raise the morale of every person who worked there.

Snyder: How did you do that?

Sakey: By talking with them. I personally set out to find the great leaders in the company. I researched who was good at what. I talked to them personally. I let them know how valuable I thought they were. And, if necessary, I put them in roles where their true talents would shine. In essence, I found it my job to let the employees know it was not their fault the company went bankrupt, and that things were going to be different.

We began a whole process around raising the corporate self-image, celebrating our profession, and raising the level of communication at every level. I also got involved in the trenches, and helped out wherever I could, even with relatively mundane tasks. I made myself available as an educator to everyone, if they needed my help. At the same time, we set about changing our view. We asked, "Who are we?" The answer to that question was simple: We are a company that is all about people, and we are all about character, commitment, and passion. We will look for and cultivate those traits in our own company, and we will help others find great employees who have those traits as well. So, in the end, an examination of character was not just a business model for bringing Headway out of bankruptcy; it became the whole philosophy upon which we set out to build a great new company, which now is experiencing both profitability and growth, across the United States, with a rejuvenated and enthusiastic workforce.

Snyder: You have learned a lot in your career about the character traits of hig-performing individuals. From all those years of observation, and all of your experiences, what do you think is most important?

Sakey: My experience in working with Headway over the past three years, and seeing its dramatic turnaround, has reinforced something I have always known, but have been strongly reminded of—you need to focus first and foremost on hiring people who have character and who are committed to getting the job done. People who have a record of character and commitment. You also have to look for the unique combination of realism and optimism. Good leaders are realistic in what can be achieved, but they are also very optimistic. In other words, they set realistic expectations but they are optimistic in how they lead. I am a very optimistic person. I believe that every person we hire is going to be the greatest person we have ever hired. I struggle at balancing my own realism with my optimism.

Another important character trait I look for is honesty. If you have bad news, you have to share it with the people whose lives are being affected by it. But not only do good leaders share bad news, they also share their plan for addressing it. The next thing I look for is persistence—people who have a record of never giving up. Everyone has had setbacks. So you need to look at a person's tenacity. A lot of failures can be attributed to people who just gave up. We all know the story of Thomas Edison, and how many types of metal he had to go through before he finally found that tungsten was going to work in that lightbulb. I also look for articulate people—people who have an ability to communicate their message. In order to lead, leaders have to be able to get other people to follow. They also have to be able to teach. They have to be caring and compassionate about that—their responsibility to teach and help others. I want to see our people succeed—I want to see them paying more taxes because they are making more money. So I look for executives who are balanced and caring. In sum, the whole attitude of caring—caring for your company and caring for your people—is one of the strongest hallmark traits of character. And that attitude of caring, in essence, is the foundation upon which I have sought to build the new Headway.

♛

A Few Additional Thoughts on the Nature of Trust

A friend and colleague of mine, Joe Healey, who has been described as one of the world's best speakers on leadership, has written an outstanding book titled *Radical Trust: How Today's Great Leaders Convert People to Partners* (Wiley, 2007).

Healey, whose consulting practice is based in Virginia Beach, Virginia, makes a compelling case, backed by numerous examples drawn from his experience as a banker, entrepreneur, and corporate consultant, that trust between managers and team members is the ultimate key to performance and productivity for all high-performing organizations.

In citing the benefits of trust, Healey offers the following pivotal insights, among others:

- High trust permits a more fulfilling workplace and generates warmth that retains and draws talent. Employees are far more likely to refer and recruit talent.

- Employees (in environments where trust exists) are more empowered to take risks and innovate.

- Employees share knowledge because they trust that their boss knows their value.

- Partnership and collaboration flourish because the primary catalyst for them is intact: leadership by example. The walls that create silos have no foundation to stand.

✗ Development occurs at a rapid pace.

✗ People universally want to be around people they trust, so work becomes a home.

In such an environment, Healey insists, trust is earned. It is not taken for granted, and it is not demanded. Just like character itself, all of those key executive traits that build a foundation of trust must be proved and demonstrated daily.

Legitimate Leadership Involves Two-Way Trust

In this chapter, we have attempted to outline some of the practical strategies and tools that can be used to source, select, hire, and promote outstanding executives and managers. Our discussion has also focused on the critical role that trust plays in the performance of all great organizations and teams.

To conclude, I would like to share a brief document that I wrote many years ago, as the result of having interviewed hundreds of successful executives as a business magazine editor in my younger days. It distills my observations on what I found were a few key traits of successful leaders. I once sent this list to an executive I was working with when I started my first consulting practice more than a decade ago, and came to find out that he had forwarded it to other executives. One day, I was visiting a company in New York and found it posted on the refrigerator in the break room.

I believe there is a strong resonance between the items on this list and one central observation I have heard from many sincere and successful leaders—the observation that trust is earned.

Here is the list:

The Seven Essential Traits of Legitimate Leaders

1. Legitimate Leaders go out of their way to support and encourage their people.

2. Legitimate Leaders go out of their way to unite people at every turn and are quick to facilitate reconciliation when they feel the team is being disunited.

3. Legitimate Leaders intermingle with their people frequently and have extensive familiarity with the problems, psychological well-being, performance, job history, and even family life of the people under their supervision. Leaders who supervise multitudes still care about the struggles of each and every one.

4. Legitimate Leaders know everything that is going on in their companies in every department and are in frequent contact with their team members, down to the lowest person on the hierarchical totem pole.

5. Legitimate Leaders encourage and seek out constant communication with staff and discourage no one from contacting them at any time.

6. Legitimate Leaders are able to gather great amounts of information because they develop the kind of supportive and noncritical relationships that cause their employees to seek them out and give them information.

7. Legitimate Leaders seldom dwell on their authority but spend most of their time trying to help solve problems and mediate conflicts, often by delegating and relinquishing power. By doing so, they are usually entrusted with huge amounts of authority. But they do not fight for it, or demand it. Their people give it to them.

These are but a few of the essential qualities that we look for advising anyone on how to source, recruit, and promote great executives and managers.

And, as time has proven, they may continue to be among the most important qualities to look for first.

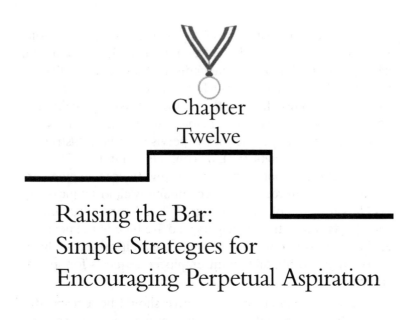

Chapter
Twelve

Raising the Bar:
Simple Strategies for
Encouraging Perpetual Aspiration

The primary reason you want to select and retain the best people is obvious: High-performing individuals are better at attracting and retaining more and better customers.

In this chapter, we will show the way combined selection and training efforts can help you build stronger teams, all the while employing simple internal strategies that will help you retain more customers and accelerate growth.

All of the lessons we will study by way of a case history in this chapter are tied in with accountability. Because the issue of accountability will be paramount, I want to take a brief moment to address an intriguing question that has been circulating of late in management circles. The question is whether enlightened managers should try to be good friends with the people they manage. On this question I have a very simple answer.

The manager must be a friendly "teacher"—approachable, helpful, and respectful—but never a friend in the conventional sense, if friendship means unconditional love and implicit favoritism. Though there is much debate on this issue, I would like to offer an insight from the real world: Workplace friendships among *peers* can be valuable, but friendships between managers and the people they supervise can be disastrous if they lead to bias, favoritism, or conflicts of interest. Furthermore, friendships between managers and their team members can make the enforcement of accountability almost impossible. As Harvard psychologist Dr. Myra White has pointed out, research has shown that managers who are high in the need for affiliation make poor managers because their need to be liked causes them to liberally grant employee requests for special treatment.

Again, the manager or executive should be a respectful coach who is a constant teacher, and one who leads by example, but friendship between a manager and team members can be risky. This risk is a critical point to consider when you are attempting to build successful teams.

In the early part of this book we discussed the specter of entitlement, which corporations must guard against at every turn. Although we have stated it before, we will state it again—there are job candidates out there who feel that the world owes them a living, and that the most important goal is to find a "comfortable" place to work where one will be taken care of. Such a mentality must be eradicated as a workplace attitude if teams are to realize that their first goal is to be accountable. Friends, as far as I understand the term, offer unconditional positive regard. They are there to listen without judgment to complaints, gripes, hurts, and excuses when the situation calls for it. If a manager develops such a relationship with a person under his or her supervision, it will be almost impossible to discuss or enforce measures of accountability.

Because most high-performing individuals are being choosy about the environments they will agree to work in, most organizations must walk a tightrope.

On one hand, organizations must do everything in their power to create working environments and business models that are based upon honest values, excellent products, and services, and respectful leadership.

However, these working environments can never be so friendly that team members lose sight of the fact that they are not there to be comfortable—they are there to prove themselves, perform, and constantly raise the bar. Building a respectful but competitive environment is easier said than done.

In the next section, I will provide a case history of one client I have worked with: the MAGIC fashion industry trade show of Advanstar Communications, which is the largest fashion industry trade show in the world, and Advanstar's most profitable business unit.

The environment of leadership and accountability at MAGIC provides an excellent example of how a company can provide a meaningful and exciting work environment, with strict measures of accountability and performance at the same time.

How Accountability Works in Paradise

MAGIC's corporate offices are nestled in the palm-tree-lined community of Woodland Hills, California, just a stone's throw from the film capital, Burbank. Twice a year, in February and August, the company takes over the Las Vegas convention center and produces the largest fashion trade show on the face of the earth. This trade show not only represents and promotes the international fashion industry, but in many ways it also helps to define it. Brand-name designers—both the famous and the up-and-coming—attend the show in order to dazzle buyers with the latest offspring of their fashion genius.

Buyers from every major retail store, large and small, attend the show in order to see what's hot, what's trendy, what the latest brands are up to, and how they are stacking up against the competition. Manufacturers of fabric, contract manufacturers, and original design manufacturers from every corner of the globe come to show their wares as well, as they mingle with those branded companies who may well end up using their fabrics, designs, or manufacturing expertise. The environment of the trade show is consummately thrilling and competitive. In every sense of the word, everyone is trying to look his or her best. Inside the brightly lit Las Vegas convention center, in rooms the size of football fields, are thousands and thousands of glimmering racks, upon which hang the shirts, dresses, coats, ties, jeans, T-shirts, belts, and earrings that will end up as new product offerings in every major retail store in the world. Circulating among the beautiful throngs of artistic mavens and hipster denizens are fabulous fashion models, celebrities, and hundreds of cool, confident young millionaires attending to their booths, dressed in $200 T-shirts and $300 jeans.

Certainly, you could not ask for a more entertaining or "fashionable" place to work. The team members of MAGIC work, interact, and consult with more people in more sectors of the fashion industry than any other company—in any area of the globe. Yet there is more to the job than just a fashionable good time. There is a tremendous amount of accountability and responsibility to both the client and the company.

That is because the clients of MAGIC—both retailers and brands—are looking to MAGIC's account executives to help them take a pulse of the industry and obtain insight on future trends. In many cases, they make critical business decisions based on the level of the market intelligence with which MAGIC team members provide them. So, when you show up at the world's largest trade show, and you witness the evolution of trends (what the fashion industry refers to as *morphing*), and you see how many of the world's most creative designers are riffing on similar themes, it becomes glaringly apparent that MAGIC does not just organize an exhibition of fashion trends; it is intimately involved in helping to communicate those trends. Staying on top of the competitive intelligence in this complex industry requires sophisticated, ongoing training efforts coupled with stringent measure of accountability for self-education, self-direction, and performance.

In the next section, we will describe the way the senior management at MAGIC work with their team members to conduct the balancing act of providing meaningful, "fashionable" work, and high levels of metric-driven accountability at the same time.

Team Meetings at MAGIC: A Behind the Scenes Look at Training and Accountability

In working with the sales, customer service, and marketing teams of MAGIC, my firm has collaborated with senior management to build and deliver training programs that help the people who work for MAGIC to be better consultants to the fashion-oriented companies and designers with which they work.

While we cannot discuss trade secrets or competitive positioning items, it should be useful for all readers to go behind the scenes with us for a moment to look at the necessity of applying a philosophy of *accuracy* and *simplicity* to all efforts aimed at employee training and customer retention. To give a sense of "being there," we will shift to the present tense.

Behind Closed Doors

So, here we are behind closed doors in the training room of MAGIC. A few doors down the hall there is a large holding room for all of the clothes that will be exhibited on the runway shows at MAGIC in February. Hundreds of hands and eyes are busy at work, as they concentrate on coordinating and staging one of the largest marketing, entertainment, and buying spectacles in the civilized world. Yet, inside this room—behind closed doors—the executives of this organization are focused on simplicity, conciseness, subject matter knowledge, and consultative credentials. At the head of the room are Laura McConnell, executive vice president, who knows the fashion industry like the back of her hand; Chris McCabe, vice president and general manager, who knows the trade show industry like the back of his hand; Camille Candella, director of marketing, who has as much hard data on the fashion trade show business as any human being working in the industry; and myself.

When Laura speaks and addresses the roomful of people from many corners of the organization—operations, sales, customer service, retail relations, marketing—she makes a simple but powerful statement.

"The most important thing you should ask yourself each morning is this," she says. "How am I different today than I was yesterday?"

In explaining what she means by "being different every day," Laura drives straight to the heart of customer service and accountability—by making it intimately *personal*. She continues:

That really is the only question that highly successful people ask themselves: How am I different today than I was yesterday? Either you care about the question or you don't. Either you have an answer, or you don't. It's that simple. And people who care about the question and the answer also have a few other simple questions they ask themselves. What new goals have I set for myself today? What have I learned? What have I set my mind on improving? How can I make myself better today than I was yesterday? In our organization, I have certain expectations of each and every one of you. I expect you to be self-motivated. I expect you to want to learn and improve. I expect that you will want to become more knowledgeable as a subject matter expert in your field every day. And if I ask you how you are different today as a professional than you were yesterday, I expect you to be able to tell me. If ask you what you new goals are, I expect you to be able to tell me. And if I ask you what you are more knowledgeable in today, I expect you to be able to tell me. I am saying all of this for a simple reason—it is because I have to know that when you get on the phone with our customers, that I can trust they will be certain that you are more knowledgeable and more valuable and more helpful to them than any other person they will talk to this week. That's the heart of our business. That's where all of our growth will come from.

After this speech, there is a moment of silence in which you can tell that some people feel excited and newly motivated, and others feel scared to death. Once the weight of these expectations has had time to sink in, Laura moves into training mode.

"Okay," she says. "In preparation for next week's training, I want to tell you a couple of competitive facts and messages that are defining the future of the fashion industry. After that, I want you to research these trends and then be prepared to tell us next week—concisely—how these trends impact your customers and your business division."

After Laura has finished her part of the training, Chris McCabe, the vice president and general manager of the show, addresses the group. Chris is here because he (similar to Laura), has also proven himself as a subject matter expert and industry leader in the trade show business. Chris, who (similar to Laura) can appear soft-spoken and friendly, is also a classic coach. He is seemingly modest and helpful on the surface, but in spite of this, he (similar to Laura) is brutal and relentless when it comes to performance. In a meeting the week before, he had summed up his plan with the following words:

"Good morning people," he said. "As you know, I have been brought to MAGIC to help achieve growth. In order to do that, we are going to do everything in our power to give you the training and the resources you need to be as successful as you can. But you have to do your part. Because there is a tough part to my job. For lack of a better expression, I have been asked to build a Super Bowl team. And that means there is no insurance you will automatically stay on this team forever."

When Chris had made this statement the week before, some people had seemed excited, and in their eyes you could tell they were thinking, "Well then, bring it on! I can take the heat!" Others, of course, looked terrified, as if they were already reading the handwriting on this wall.

This morning Chris has a notepad in his hand. And this is how he addresses the group:

> We asked each one of you to prepare a three-minute memorized speech in which you have to address the room and tell us, in your own words, and using the most powerful data you have available, what makes us vastly superior to the competition, and what your customers have to know if they are to dominate the market this year. Camille, Laura, David, and myself have been feeding you data for two months. Now you have three minutes. I will be taking notes on the points you made and the points you missed. Your goal is to astonish me—and to make me feel that you are offering an opportunity that I cannot live without.

The group that was being graded here on their ability to accurately communicate the company's key competitive messages had also been assessed on workplace competencies using validated instruments. And for the salespeople, data was captured, naturally, on how close they had come to meeting targets. In addition, the director of marketing, Camille

Candella, had given a numeric grade on her perception of the quality of SWOT analyses done for each salesperson's main competitor in the market. Each salesperson, that is, was asked to do a SWOT analysis comparing MAGIC's competitive advantages to the competition on a spreadsheet using the kind of simple formula we have discussed in previous chapters.

One interesting aspect of the grades Chris gave to the presentation format just described is that there was an evident correlation, however rough, between the scores that individuals made on their competitive speeches, and the results they had received not only on validated assessment tests of skill and "sales character," but also on the exercises that required them to read, study, and take notes in previous training sessions.

After having studied the results of implementing multiphased training and assessment programs at numerous companies, it has become clear to me that high-achieving individuals in the workplace seem to have similar and predictable traits that show up time and time again, whenever they are assessed or given challenging assignments. The following observations, I believe, are key to understanding how we go about assessing, building, and developing "intelligent" teams.

+ When high-achieving individuals are in meetings, they demonstrate a zeal for learning, and take a lot of notes.

+ High-performing individuals get their assignments in on time at the bare minimum, and usually long before they are due.

+ When high-performing individuals are given a chance to demonstrate their excellence before others, they almost always come over-prepared and bend over backwards to exceed expectations.

✦ When high-performing individuals write or speak about their last employer, they will usually praise their previous employer, and talk about passionate commitments they made and successes they enjoyed. In some legitimate cases, high-performing individuals may have been abused in a previous job, but in more cases than not, the attitude of exuberance they demonstrate in their current job has been a pattern and attitude throughout their careers.

✦ High-performing individuals are usually more concise, fact-based, and articulate when discussing their goals and strategies. That is because they spend more time studying and planning, and are generally more prepared for success than others. It comes through in everything they do.

✦ The traits reflected in these points usually show through in competency-based assessment tests, which tend to show that higher performing people in many professions are more organized, more self-reliant, more dependable, and more optimistic than others.

Putting the Big Picture Under a Microscope

As I have noticed in my firm's work with cutting-edge companies such as Advanstar, there is a link between simplicity and innovation that is often misunderstood: The best ideas usually are simple—they are not difficult to understand, they are easy to explain, and once embraced by the right team, they are a cinch to implement. If implemented properly, they are usually profitable as well. However—and this is the hard part for some to grasp—simplicity takes a long time to perfect.

Moreover, the type of ideas that drive a company forward are always tied to a burning vision, and the best visions are always created collaboratively by businesspeople and business teams that have a relentless desire to be better today than they were yesterday. In this light, all training programs designed for high achievers must be personal, and they must challenge the individual to aspire to greater levels of excellence. In other words, great training programs always help to waken employees from their slumber, and cause them to become dissatisfied with current levels of performance. But—and this is important—the process of helping people see how they can become better, and why they *must* become better, cannot and does not happen overnight. The process has to be methodical and deliberate.

For example, one of the most important competitive considerations for MAGIC and other units of Advanstar is the development of new initiatives—new targets, approaches, or concepts that might attract more and better customers because they are better in tune with the market.

The goal then is to come up with beautifully simple initiatives that can be sold and implemented rather quickly. But you can't just walk up to people and ask them to come up with beautifully simple initiatives that will sell and make money. You have to prime their brains for innovative thinking first.

Everything we have talked about in this chapter (and in the entire book, for that matter) has been about helping to prime the brains of team members to think the way champions do—in the context of simple, meaningful, and purposeful plans they can put the full strength of their minds and hearts behind. Here is another way to look at it: If the company is to be different and better next quarter than it was this quarter, all individuals must be challenged on a daily basis to be better than they were yesterday, the organization must hire managers and executives who are worthy to teach, and people must be held accountable for their progress once they have been given the benefit of the classroom.

Here is a portion of a simple worksheet we have used with some teams, with most of the questions leading back to the simple but powerful principle of personal "difference-making."

———

1. What is the most significant action or change you plan to make this quarter to differentiate yourself and become more successful as a businessperson/business category owner?

    _____

2. What is the most exciting and potentially profitable new initiative you would like to help create and put into place next quarter?

    _____

3. What are your target goals for next quarter?

    _____

4. Do you feel you understand your own track record?

    _____

5. What is your track record?

    _____

6. How do you plan to push yourself next quarter?

    _____

7. What is an acceptable level of growth for you?

    _____

8. Based on what you have in your database, do you have enough targets to succeed?

    _____

9. How can we help you get more targets?

_____

Most business owners will realize that these are important questions for many teams and individuals. However, in looking for answers to these questions, it is important that you not ask your people to give their responses too readily.

The best, most simple, and most profitable answers to these questions most often come after a trial by fire—after you have asked people to prove their passion, their intent to study, their desire to always do their best in front of their peers, their desire to somehow always be just a little bit better today than they were yesterday. In this context it is often useful to give your potential high performers tough assignments and rigorous training, if only to see what they will do with it all. Tough assignments and high expectations almost always motivate high performers to come forward with creative solutions for competitive challenges. When employees with high levels of entitlement are given tough assignments, they usually do nothing but complain. In the end, the fastest way to build intelligent teams is to put forth high expectations. Once you set these higher expectations, and bring the entire organization together as a single, united teaching unit for those who do desire to learn and become better every day, you will begin to see your company's best ideas emerge, take hold, and grow.

How Leaders Can Work at Change: Key Questions

As the preceding sections have attempted to demonstrate, companies that are passionate about and committed to selection, retention, and development ask star players to constantly put themselves under a microscope with regard to self-improvement goals.

But, as we have discussed, great leaders also put themselves under the microscope on a regular basis, and take the time to examine their own developmental needs so that they can be in a better position to teach others.

Rick Rocchetti, manager of organization development and training for the City of Raleigh, North Carolina, has written an excellent article entitled "Leaders Who Work at Change Can Change Work" (*Employment Relations Today,* Wiley Periodicals, Inc., Summer 2006).

In this paper Rocchetti makes the following pivotal and succinct observation: "Leadership is about the decision to become more human. It is about bringing forth my character and developing my competence as much as it is about dealing with the external environment."

In describing how leaders conduct their own process of ruthless self-examination, Rocchetti provides a long list of important questions that leaders must ask of themselves when facing any important change that is occurring, or must occur, inside of their organizations.

Just a few of them are:

- ✦ What are you trying to achieve at this time of your life? How does this change affect your life?

- ✦ How do you see your role as a leader? How will this change challenge that?

- ✦ What is the conversation you need to have with yourself that you are not currently having?

- ✦ What choices do you need to make in order to shift your attention to be able to deal with this change?

- ✦ Are you the right person to take this organization through this change? Is this the right time?

- ✦ If a vocation is where your "deepest joy connects with the world's deepest need," where is that for you? Is it in alignment with where you are right now?

✦ Where is your internal resistance? Where are you in dissent with yourself? How can you make the space to have the conversation?

✦ What assumptions are you making? Are these consistent with organizational assumptions? Should other assumptions be examined? If so, which ones? Would outcomes be different if you didn't make these assumptions?

Back to Moral Intelligence

The type of fearless self-examination suggested by Rocchetti is thematically consistent with the type of fearless "moral inventory" truthfulness outlined by Lennick and Kiel in their book *Moral Intelligence*, which we have cited many times.

Interestingly, a significant number of the questions listed in Lennick and Kiel's "Moral Competency Inventory" are remarkably well aligned with the competencies or "character traits" of high-performing individuals—traits such as being honest with oneself, having follow-through and interest in other people, and being helpful.

Here are but a few statements leaders are prompted to consider in the Moral Competency Inventory:

✦ I can clearly state the principles, values, and beliefs that guide my actions.

✦ I tell the truth, unless there is an overriding reason to withhold it.

✦ I will generally confront someone if I see him or her doing something that isn't right.

✦ When I agree to do something, I always follow through.

✦ When I make a decision that turns out to be a mistake, I admit it.

✦ I own up to my mistakes and failures.

✦ My colleagues would say I go out of my way to help them.

✦ My first response when I meet new people is to be genuinely interested in them.

The simple but solid value behind such character-oriented statements proves once again that studying character in oneself or in one's organization does not have to be viewed as an abstract or impossibly philosophical task.

In most instances, great leaders implicitly understand that character improvement is an immensely practical affair. Benjamin Franklin made a list of traits he wanted to improve (most of them character traits), and worked on them ceaselessly. One at a time.

Viewing character improvement at the individual and organizational level as a practical concern, one might ask the question: How do I most effectively go about improving the character of my organization, or the character of myself?

One simple response might be: Ask your leaders to take the Moral Competency Inventory, find a few traits they would like to improve, and then get them to explain to you how they plan to go about improving those traits throughout the next few months. Or, using the Moral Competency Inventory as a guide, along with the resources in this book, you might construct another list of questions for yourself that are tied with the character traits you feel are most important for success. Using your own list, what do you want to work on first?

Some critics may point out that it is impossible to improve character in an organization or an individual because the most important character traits are either innate or ingrained by the time a person becomes an adult.

Even if it is or might be true that character becomes cemented by adulthood, that does not undermine the value of our proposition. Character can always be improved by individuals who have character to begin with. This is a concept well recognized by the Marines, and a theme we have been following since the beginning of this book. A person without character would not even bother to take the time with a Moral Competency Inventory. But a person with high character will make this kind of self-examination and self-development second nature.

Therefore, if we spend more time selecting, hiring, and developing these kinds of individuals, then we can be guaranteed that we will not only build more intelligent teams, but will also make daily, monthly, quarterly, and yearly improvements to the character of our companies.

In this light, putting a greater value on character in hiring and development must certainly be a part of "moral intelligence" as well.

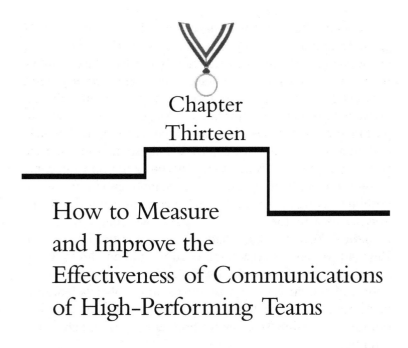

Chapter
Thirteen

How to Measure and Improve the Effectiveness of Communications of High-Performing Teams

In the previous chapter, we discussed simple strategies for raising the bar—building teams that are composed of individuals who have clear plans for increasing their professional skills on that team, and whose action plans are encouraged and supported by great managers.

As we demonstrated, you cannot build or sustain intelligent teams without clear communications. Yet these clear communications must not only come from management consistently—they must also be omnipresent in and among teams. Because without the presence of clear communications internally, there will always be poor communications externally with customers.

Because so many corporations are interested in how to measure and improve internal and external communications, and because the quality of communications is so critical to both employee retention and customer retention, we will dedicate this chapter to that subject.

Much of the material in this chapter draws from the background and expertise of my colleague Sid Reynolds, who is CEO of the Signature Agency in Raleigh, North Carolina, a public relations and marketing firm (see *www.signatureagency.com*). Sid herself is certainly one of those high-performing individuals we have discussed in this book. Among many other accomplishments, she was an editor at Harcourt Brace Jovanovich, and then editorial director at a trade publishing firm when she was only in her 20s. Since then, she has gone on to become recognized as a leading expert on communication metrics in both marketing efforts and internal communications efforts. Serving as director of communications psychology for the Signature Agency, I have had the opportunity to work with Reynolds on improved communications and employee development projects for our clients. Following is a thorough explanation of the current best practices and tools available for measuring and improving internal and external communications as a front-line strategy for both employee and customer retention.

Best Practices in Internal Marketing: Strategies for Building Continuous Planned Momentum

Once you build a high-performing team, the process of creating powerful momentum within your organization hinges on how well your front-line ambassadors understand and trust your organizational vision.

As a result, a critical component of leadership momentum is ensuring that the capable team members you work so hard to hire—individuals who bring valuable character and commitment to your organization—remain focused on the big picture.

As Reynolds has described this to her own clients for decades, the vehicle you use to ensure that your hand-picked recruits understand and trust your vision is, of course, internal communications. In fact, internal communications is the sinew of organizational health and business success, because it spans all your enterprises and quickly becomes inseparable from your corporate culture. In addition to leading change through all levels of your organization, communications allows you to motivate employees to think about the bottom line, drive service performance, prevent crisis, and communicate to a diverse workforce with a consistent voice.

In the 2006 Internal Marketing Best Practices study, conducted by graduate students of the integrated marketing communications department at Northwestern University, six characteristics that drive internal goal-driven success were clearly identified:

1. Senior management participation.
2. Integrated organizational structure.
3. Strategic marketing approach.
4. Human resources partnership.
5. Focus on employee engagement.
6. Internal brand communication.

Despite internal branding's value, institutions implement complex recruitment, hiring, and ongoing training procedures, yet often fail to prioritize a solid internal branding program, Reynolds has observed. In fact, because internal communications falls under the scope of employee relations, human resources professionals rely on traditional tools, such as the periodic newsletter and centrally located bulletin boards, to maintain contact with all employees. When marketing communicators are included for tactical support, they supply an annual recognition event with materials or perhaps install a monthly open-mike session with the COO or CEO, and focus the rest of their time, enthusiasm, and budget on external communications. In the end, managers of internal communications list birthdays and employment anniversary dates, and too often forget to mention changes in sustainable process. Meanwhile, the newest social media tools, innovation, and brain science creativity are saved for external branding efforts. Internal communications is seldom viewed as an opportunity to invigorate unstoppable successes.

The Importance of Reinforcing Messages

"Employees, like all message customers, need to hear or see the same message over and over again before it can be retained and acted upon," Reynolds argues. "As any [receiver of messages], employees vacuum up information differently. Although some retain content more quickly by hearing the message from their supervisor and others by seeing it in writing, an impressive number needs to interact with the experience of others before attitudes can change. These employees need 'permission' to trust corporate plans. Most employees need to connect with the message in multiple formats before it sticks undistorted."

In fact, Reynolds points out, successful internal communications programs are designed to manage momentum with a steady drumbeat that echoes blockbuster consumer product campaign strategy. In these internal programs, communicators:

- Verify that the leaders are in alignment before they go public with a new mantra. The CEO, CFO, and department heads are the spokespersons, and must reinforce the talk with visible action.

- Make sure the facts make sense. If any of the facts don't seem believable, the toll on trust is devastating. Successful communicators take the time to ensure that the important leaders agree on the truth, and that the message seems honest.

- ✖ Give background. If leaders don't provide the background, they can rest assured that a revised factual background will be invented—without their involvement. Organizations are made up of persons, and persons, by nature, want to feel important. Knowledge is leverage. Once people are given the background from the leadership, distortions are less necessary, because, often, repeating the just-reviewed message catapults the individual's sense of self-worth and satisfies the need to seem "in-the-know."

- ✖ Protect the messages against too much complexity. Even highly educated audiences respond more quickly to a simple structure with concrete information. When leaders speak academically, bullet points can break up the complexity and help audiences digest and absorb the real content, without skipping key words, and without the unintended consequence of misinformation.

- ✖ Don't allow pauses. When internal branding professionals have gaps in information flow, they realize their audience tends to manage the message by inserting a new, improved definition of the challenge and perception of appropriate next steps, which establishes a strong foundation for leadership failure.

- ✖ Say it again and again. Even though as excellent communicators tire of hearing the message, they know their audiences are absorbing it for the first time, so they REPEAT, REPEAT, REPEAT. They consider different ways to present the same information to keep the message fresh, but they keep the message out there until they know they've reached critical mass—and then they repeat the message in a steady rhythm, maybe semi weekly or monthly, just to ensure that they sustain momentum. For example, they may provide information in a newsletter, schedule an intranet exchange, add payroll envelope inserts, and schedule time for team briefings. They schedule each message event, and keep the information flowing.

✖ Pay attention to "what's in it for me." These communicators keep in mind that each audience needs the message to be tailored for selfish interest so that all individuals will know how any policy change will affect them.

✖ Brief the department heads in writing, relying on a steady, predictable update schedule.

✖ Ensure feedback mechanisms. One-way communication doesn't work in today's business culture; therefore, smart marketers don't fight that reality. They ensure that audiences feel they have the privilege of convenient conversation with leadership.

How Communication Failure Occurs

Documented failures, from medication errors in hospitals to overspent budgets in building projects, are born from misunderstandings. Misunderstandings tend to occur at eight connection levels:

1. Information silos between a board and the administration.

2. Information silos between the administration and department heads.

3. Communication breaks between department heads and their direct reports (the supervisors).

4. Communication breaks between competing department heads.

5. Communication breaks between supervisor and support team.

6. Communication breaks due to employee/manager absence at the time of important announcements.

7. Communication gaps between supplier and organization.

8. Communication gaps between organization and customer or customer advocates.

As a result, communications initiatives should address all eight connection/tension levels. The challenge is to take a look at each of the eight connection levels through the perception of each stakeholder group, and then work to inform each group—and the whole organization—frequently enough that each group believes your message is consistent across enterprises, and yet believes your message is clear and important to the group. In the end, you obtain the results you need only by providing a consistent message several different ways via several media vehicles.

Summary: Key Benefits of Improved Communications Processes

As communications experts such as Reynolds have demonstrated, the key goal of improving internal and external communications is to reduce the risk of misunderstandings and increase the awareness of system-wide standards and ideas. Both communications and functional isolation tend to lead to cascading problems. Administrators often realize they have multiple organizations that happen to be linked by a single logo and primary brand name. They have an "umbrella" system, and then they have mostly independent business units—the working departments. Quite often, department heads and shift supervisors behave as if big-picture strategic improvements at the system level really aren't connected to their departments at all.

As Reynolds reports through numerous studies with her clients, the poor coordination of messaging affects every accomplishment or innovation that makes great organizations thrive. Improvements become initiated independently at the micro-system level. But even if a smart, committed supervisor implements a brilliant solution to a problem, critical mass is never reached because it isn't shared. The great idea doesn't accomplish system-level impact due to the breakdown in linkage. In the end, competent managers may have long lists of worthy projects. Still, if administrative champions don't know they exist, excellent projects struggle for funding and fade away as soon as one detail derails or a new pet project surfaces.

But when executives from administration, human resources, and marketing communications embrace internal communications as if they were truly focused on branding system behavior and attitudes to all employees, they learn the bottom-line benefits are significant—faster goal attainment, improved product/service quality, impressive stakeholder satisfaction assessments, and reduced turnover.

In the final analysis, the keys to implementing successful alignment with your new (as well as long-term) employees and measuring the success of your internal branding are to isolate where communications can make a difference, and then employ a number of different communications tools to drive your message frequently to your teams.

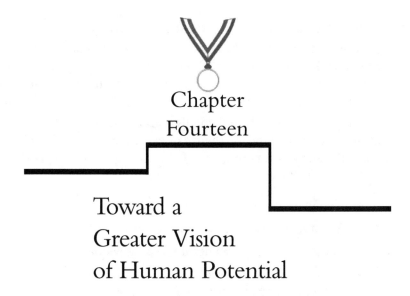

Chapter
Fourteen

Toward a
Greater Vision
of Human Potential

A few years ago, J.P. Sakey, CEO of Headway Corporate Resources, made an inspiring comment that still rings in my ears today. He stated that those of us in the human capital industry are in the "Noble Profession"—noble because we focus on the importance and the value of jobs within the context of a person's life and the life of a business. We have important work to do that does change people's lives—work that changes their standard of income and raises their standard of living. We also change the lives of companies by helping them to find the right employees that become important contributors or influencers within the organization. In the following section, I will borrow from an essay that Sakey and I wrote on this subject.

Skills of the Noble Profession Defined

As would a good psychologist or coach, any human capital professional worth his or her salt takes the time to form an in-depth relationship with every client or individual that crosses his or her professional path.

When working with individuals who are seeking a better job or looking to improve their careers, human capital professionals seek answers to many of the same questions a good psychologist will explore:

+ To what does the individual aspire?
+ What kind of talent defines the individual?
+ What kind of passion defines the individual?
+ What are the obstacles that are holding the individual back in terms of fulfilling aspirations or making the most of innate talent?
+ What can the individual do to overcome those obstacles?
+ How can the human capital professional help him or her to overcome those obstacles?

When we say that our profession is "noble," we mean that it is noble when professionals in our industry are truly living up to their responsibility, putting the needs of the individual and client first, and doing everything in their power to achieve the goal of helping individuals overcome any and all obstacles to their personal growth, fulfillment and career development.

That also takes the impact of our profession one step beyond psychology. Like good psychologists or coaches, professionals in our industry can listen with sensitivity to the setbacks, frustrations, obstacles, and thwarted dreams that have affected everyone from the candidate through his or her employer, to his or her family members, friends, and loved ones.

Perhaps the most important thing that people in our profession can do to help other people change their lives in the most significant way is to help them find the right job. But not just *any* job—a job that helps individuals *and* the companies they work for to better themselves by providing a perfect match between individual aspirations and company goals.

The achievement of that perfect match between aspiring individuals and aspiring companies will never happen, however, without a great deal of thoughtful analysis and consummate dedication to the skill sets required of people working in the "noble profession." It does not work when you thoughtlessly shovel people into companies and situations in which they do not belong—this only hurts the individual and the companies that hire them. Yes, it may be more difficult to work harder in this profession, to listen more carefully and more scientifically to the needs of candidates and clients, to methodically study the needs of all the people concerned, and then make educated and knowledgeable recommendations that put the genuine interests of others before your own. But if you are to hold your head up and say that you are a member of the noble profession, that is what you must do; you must slow down, you must listen, you must evaluate, and you must judge. And in your judgments you must always ask if you have done everything in your power to bring your candidates and your clients one step closer to success.

Here are a few more observations on the nature of human potential and professional excellence that I think you will find inspiring.

Just as I was finishing this book, I had the opportunity to speak at length with Doug Lennick, coauthor of *Moral Intelligence*, managing partner of the Lennick Aberman Group, and an executive vice president with Ameriprise. We were discussing the issue of whether one's character becomes cemented in stone at some point. Lennick made a thoughtful observation that I think will serve as an excellent conclusion to this book. But first, just a little more background on Lennick's credentials in the area of leadership development.

As has been discussed earlier, Lennick is known worldwide for his expertise in driving business results by helping managers and businesspeople improve their emotional intelligence skills. At Ameriprise, Lennick continues to work directly with the leadership team, focusing on workplace culture and performance. In every sense of the word, he is one of those high-performing individuals we have described in the course of this book. He has supervised, coached, or mentored more than 17,000 other high-performing individuals in his career. Because of Lennick's genuine leadership and credentials, I find his vision of human potential to be both important and poignant. In the following paragraphs, I will try to encapsulate the inspiring point he made when we were on the phone.

Citing cutting-edge research in neuroscience, Lennick suggested that human beings are not limited by anything outside of their own desire to grow. Because new research suggests that our brains are infinitely adaptable (and capable of "rewiring" to some extent), we are all works in progress throughout our lives, he proposed. In other words, we are constantly evolving, and forever empowered to become great and useful people, no matter what may have happened to us in our past, and no matter what misconceptions we may have had about our potential. The only real secret to greatness is this: We have to believe that we are capable of greatness, and respect our potential enough to do something about it.

In this light, we are all champions, every single one of us—if only we choose to be. In choosing to have the highest respect for our potential, and taking the daily actions that are necessary to sustain this success, however, I believe there are a few "secrets" that champions know and practice all of the time.

For starters, I profoundly agree with Lennick's theory that forgiveness is a central moral competency associated with people who end up leading the happiest lives and leaving the biggest mark on the world.

There is a tremendous amount of suffering in the world, at times, and all of us experience painful circumstances and emotions when we come into contact with people who seem to have a lack of character—be it a lack of concern for others, a lack of concern for themselves, a lack of honesty, or a lack of compassion and helpfulness.

To reiterate: I believe it is true that forgiveness is an essential component of success in these difficult and challenging times that we live in, because without forgiveness, we are bound to spend an inordinate amount of our mental energy nursing the wounds of injuries and painful circumstances that we often had no control over to begin with. Champion individuals are undoubtedly the type of people who focus first and foremost on the things that they *can* change—and choose not to worry about the events or situations that are beyond their control. By choosing to take actions of forgiveness, for example, champions are able to liberate themselves from the emotional and psychological bonds that hold other people back.

There is another interesting component associated with high-achieving individuals—the trait of integrity, as manifested by a desire to always do the right thing, as much as humanly possible. Interestingly enough, this trait shows up in an important study done by Lennick's colleagues on the traits of high-performing financial advisors, those who deliver the best returns for their clients. ("Morally and Emotionally Competent Financial Advisors Deliver Superior Client Service and Portfolio Performance," Aberman, et al. See bibliography.)

The findings are enlightening, and may provide a roadmap for success and excellence in many other fields as well.

Results from the research of Lennick and his colleagues on the performance of financial advisors demonstrated that the following competencies were most statistically important.

Integrity was identified as the key behavioral competency that predicted the most positive returns for clients.

Other traits demonstrated as most important were:

+ Client service orientation.
+ Concern for order/quality.
+ Teamwork.
+ Self-confidence.
+ Achievement orientation.

In this book, we have discussed the high value of putting an emphasis on character as one way to predict performance in selection. The research by Lennick's associates, just cited as an example, seems to be a perfect reminder of this philosophy. Again, character—in the form of integrity—comes through first.

In my view, it may well be that this core trait of integrity is possibly a master trait that gives rise to and strengthens other traits of high-quality service delivery. Essentially, commitment and high-quality service delivery distinguishes many high-performing individuals in many professions.

It also seems obvious to me that character—exemplified by integrity and the other traits we have described in this book—creates the essential self-confidence and purpose that enables almost all other success-oriented traits to flourish.

As I reached out to several notable executives to get their views on the key traits of success in business, I received a thoughtful reply from Roger Horchow, a Broadway producer, prolific author, and the founder of the Horchow Collection, the famous luxury mail-order catalog business that was eventually sold to Neiman Marcus.

These were the simple words he had to offer about the most important principles involved in achieving success: "I guess honesty, willingness to admit a mistake, knowing when to praise, learning how to offer criticism in a constructive way, knowing your subordinates as people rather than job functionaries, sharing good news and bad news, and developing a team. Share the profits if you can. Set a good example in charitable works and financial activities, and volunteer. Stand for something!"

That last sentence seems to encapsulate a lot of what we have tried to discuss here.

What is it that you stand for?

And no matter what has happened to you in the past, how do you plan to let the world know that you care about this thing in the depths of your soul?

And once you know the answer to that, what do you plan to do about it today, tomorrow, and the day after that?

As champions, or potential champions, we are supposed to address these issues every day. And, as employers, we are simply supposed to do all we can to continuously encourage the people who work for us, so that they will want to keep answering those questions with spirit, resolve, character, commitment, passion, and joy.

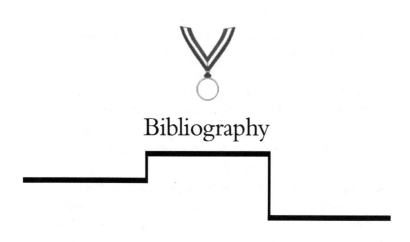

Bibliography

Aberman, Rick, Judy Skoglund, Chuck Wachendorfer, Kris Petersen, Robert J. Emmerling, and Lyle Spencer. "Morally and Emotionally Competent Financial Advisors Deliver Superior Client Service and Portfolio Performance." White Paper, Lennick Aberman Group, May 2007.

Badaracco, Joseph L., Jr. "The Discipline of Building Character." *Harvard Business Review*, March–April, 1998.

Boggs, Bill. *Got What It Takes? Successful People Reveal How They Made It to the Top*. New York: HarperCollins, 2007.

Buckingham, Marcus, and Curt Coffman. *First Break All The Rules: What the World's Greatest Managers Do Differently*. New York: Simon and Schuster, 1999.

Carnegie, Dale. *How to Win Friends and Influence People*. New York: Pocket Books, 1936.

Collins, Jim. *Good to Great: Why Some Companies Make the Leap...and Others Don't*. New York: Harper Business, 2001.

Collins, Jim, and Jerry I. Porras. *Built to Last: Successful Habits of Visionary Companies*. New York: Harper Business Essentials, 2002.

Covey, Stephen. *The 8th Habit: From Effectiveness to Greatness*. Florence, Mass.: Free Press, 2004.

Davila, Lori, and Louise Kursmark. *How to Choose the Right Person for the Right Job Every Time*. Columbus, Ohio: McGraw-Hill, 2005.

Dellana, Scott, and David P. Snyder. "Student Future Outlook and Counseling Quality in a Rural Minority High School." *High School Journal* 88(1):27–41, 2004.

Florida, Richard. *The Rise of the Creative Class: And How It's Transforming Work, Leisure, Community and Everyday Life*. New York: Perseus Book Group, 2002.

Fry, Ron. *Ask the Right Questions, Hire the Best People*. Franklin Lakes, N.J.: Career Press, 2006.

Healey, Joe. *Radical Trust: How Today's Great Leaders Convert People to Partners*. Hoboken, N.J.: Wiley, 2007.

Jacobs, Gregg. D, and David P. Snyder. "Frontal Brain Asymmetry Predicts Emotional Styles In Men." *Behavioral Neuroscience*, February 1996.

Katzenbach, Jon. *Peak Performance: Aligning the Hearts and Minds of Your Employees*. Harvard, Mass.: Harvard Business School Press, 2000.

Kouzes, James M., and Barry Z. Posner. *The Leadership Challenge: How to Keep Getting Extraordinary Things Done in Organizations*. San Francisco: Jossey-Bass Pfeiffer, 2003.

Lennick, Doug, and Fred Kiel, PhD. *Moral Intelligence: Enhancing Business Performance & Leadership Success*. Upper Saddle River, N.J.: Wharton School Publishing, 2005.

Lucia, Anntoinette D., and Richard Lepsinger. *The Art and Science of Competency Models: Pinpointing Critical Success Factors in Organizations*. San Francisco: Jossey-Bass Pfeiffer, 1999.

McCain, John, and Mark Salter. *Character Is Destiny: Inspiring Stories Every Young Person Should Know and Every Adult Should Remember*. New York: Random House, 2005.

Peterson, Christopher, and Martin Seligman. *Character Strengths and Virtues: A Handbook and Classification*. Oxford, Mass.: Oxford University Press, 2004.

Phillips, Jack. J., and Adele O. Connell. *Managing Employee Retention: A Strategic Accountability Approach*. Burlington, Mass.: Elsevier Butterworth Heinemann, 2003.

Ray, Paul H., and Sherry Ruth Anderson. *The Cultural Creatives*. New York: Harmony Books, 2000.

Rocchetti, Rick. "Leaders Who Work at Change Can Change Work." *Employment Relations Today* 33 (2), Summer 2006.

Schmidt, Frank L., and John E. Hunter. "The Validity and Utility of Selection Methods in Personnel Psychology: Practical and Theoretical Implications of 85 Years of Research Findings." *Psychological Bulletin* 124 (2): 262–274, September 1998.

Seligman, Martin. *Authentic Happiness: Using the New Positive Psychology to Realize Your Potential for Lasting Fulfillment*. Florence, Mass.: Free Press, 2002.

———. *Learned Optimism: How to Change Your Mind and Your Life*. New York: Pocket Books, 1992.

Smart, Bradford. *Topgrading: How Leading Companies Win by Hiring, Coaching, and Keeping the Best People, Revised and Updated Edition*. New York: Portfolio Hardcover, 2005.

Snyder, David P. *How to Mind-Read Your Customers*. New York: AMACOM (American Management Association), 2001.

Spranger, Eduard. *Types of Men*. Tübingen, Germany: Max Niemeyer Verlag, 1928.

Stanley, Thomas J. *The Millionaire Mind*. Riverside, N.J.: Andrews McMeel, 2000.

Turknett, Robert L., and Carolyn Turknett. *Decent People, Decent Company: How to Lead with Character at Work and in Life*. Mountain View, Calif.: Davies Black, 2005.

White, M.S. *Follow the Yellow Brick Road: A Harvard Psychologist's Guide to Becoming a Superstar*. Bonita Springs, Fla.: Work Intelligence, Inc., 2007.

Index

About the Author

DAVID **S**NYDER is founder and CEO of Snyder, Inc., a consulting firm based in Raleigh, North Carolina, and works nationwide on staff development, employment, and assessment initiatives for numerous corporations. Mr. Snyder specializes in competency-based team building, assessment, and selection across a wide spectrum of industries. He holds a master of liberal arts degree in psychology from Harvard University and is a partner with VantagePoint, Inc., a leading assessment firm based in Omaha, Nebraska. He is recognized as an expert in developing sophisticated recruiting, selection, and training models, and has served as a consultant to Headway Corporate Resources, a national staffing firm. Currently, he is concentrating on developing superior selection and training processes for the banking and financial services industries. His first book, *How to Mind-Read Your Customers*, was listed among the best books of the year by *Sales and Marketing Management Magazine* the year of its release (2001), and has since gone into translation.

To contact David Snyder regarding any of the topics in this book, including samples of validated selection tools to enhance productivity and performance in most industries, e-mail dsnyder@mindread.net, or call (919) 920-0551. Visit the Website *www.mindread.net*.